MAD HUNGRY CRAVINGS

Lucinda Scala Quinn

PHOTOGRAPHS BY
Jonathan Lovekin

ARTISAN

NEW YORK

Published by Artisan
A division of Workman Publishing Company, Inc.
225 Varick Street
New York, NY 10014-4381
artisanbooks.com

Published simultaneously in Canada by Thomas Allen & Son, Limited

★

Library of Congress Cataloging-in-Publication Data
Scala Quinn, Lucinda.
Mad hungry cravings / Lucinda Scala Quinn.
    p. cm.
Includes index.
ISBN 978-1-57965-438-2
1. Cooking. I. Title.
TX714.S3155 2013
641.5—dc23

2012010032

★

Design adapted from Jennifer S. Muller and Nick Caruso

Printed in China

First printing, February 2013

1 3 5 7 9 10 8 6 4 2

contents

INTRODUCTION

Crave it. Order it. Eat. Repeat. How could I, as a cook, or as a mom, possibly compete? Takeout meals are just too easy—especially when we're busy. And even when we're not busy, cooking can seem so hard, liable to be derailed by the smallest inconvenience. Don't have that six-ounce can of tomato paste? Better order in, eat out, get it to go, nuke it, toast it, reheat it—or just add water.

It's instinctual to yearn for the food of our mothers' and grandmothers' tables, but it may be the foods encountered in the outside world that hold the most sway over our imaginations. I've fed three sons good old-fashioned home cooking day in and day out for more than twenty-five years. Yet, to a boy, as soon as they were old enough to stray from my apron strings, out they walked—down the elevator, out of the building, and up the block to Broadway, where a whole new table of food awaited them. The fabulous New York City streets were a place of convenience and independence from their we-cook-at-home parents.

And so it was that a bowl of homemade steel-cut oats couldn't hold a candle to the delicious instant gratification of bacon, egg, and cheese on a roll at the corner deli, or else tamales from the lady near the subway. After school, a wide range of snacks tempted my boys: pastry from Starbucks, shawarma from the halal truck, hot dogs from Gray's Papaya, fried rice Chinese takeout, or, inevitably, a McDonald's Big Mac and fries.

Often they would fill themselves up before dinner but not really nourish themselves. As a cook and a mom, that really annoyed me. But part of me also gets it: I will never forget my first fast-food French fry, eaten with the babysitter when my parents went out. It was a clever plan, while it lasted, to divert child-me with a boxed burger and fries while Mom and Dad parked me and my brothers with the sitter.

Back then, the suburb of Detroit where I grew up certainly didn't have the many ethnic options of twenty-first-century New York City, but my mom was known to occasionally succumb to the lures of convenience cooking, like the TV dinner. Salisbury steak, mashed potatoes, creamed spinach, and apple-cherry cobbler—all neatly tucked into a divided aluminum container—was served once a week on TV tables. My brothers and I loved it!

So how to reconcile these two distinct notions—that we should be eating home-cooked healthy meals, but we also lust to eat things we want and crave? In my resolve to regularly make fresh-cooked food for my kids, I had an epiphany: Copy the food that you want to order in or eat out. Make it tastier and more nourishing. Any time a hankering hits, you're a well-stocked fridge or pantry away from preparing it in your own kitchen.

You know that sloppy, dog-eared file almost every family has of their takeout menus? The thing you desperately riffle through on Tuesday night at six thirty, while hollering out, "Do we want pad thai, General Tso's chicken, or Grandma's pizza?" Well, thanks to the recipes in this book, that file's days will be numbered. Granted, ordering out now and then is a welcome break from the everyday routine of cooking. But remember that home cooking has a lot more value than just the nutritional kind—especially when the bill from ordering in Chinese food is equivalent to half the week's grocery budget. (And that's to say nothing of the unwelcome side effect of puffy fingers, dry mouth, or a tummy ache from the loads of salt, sugar, and preservatives often added to the take-out food.) The sesame chicken you make at home (see page 174), will let you have what you crave, at home, but for less money and with more flavor.

how did we get there?

The fast-food economy over the past half century has dramatically changed our home lives from those of our grandparents and their grandparents. Nourishing ourselves and our families in the preindustrialized home meant planning for the growing, preserving, and cooking of our food on a daily, seasonal basis. But for the last few decades the leap from planting a seed, nurturing its growth, harvesting, cooking, and eating its fruit has been a heck of a giant one.

To many moms' credit, they persevered with simple home cooking over the years—even though the modern conveniences were alluring. Meanwhile, newer fangled prepackaged and engineered foods continued to grab our attention. Yet still, it's a privileged few across socioeconomic lines who routinely eat fresh-cooked food regularly made with good wholesome ingredients.

For many of us today, cooking has largely been handed over to distant high-volume food manufacturers—whether it's procured from a fast-food chain, a restaurant, or the grocery store shelf. Mass-produced food on this scale doesn't mean a cook is chopping onions or peeling tomatoes before they go into the industrial-sized kettle to simmer into a sanitized "meal."

Instead, prechopped produce originates from several different specialized suppliers; the onions and garlic from one distributor, mushrooms and broccoli from another. Vegetables—otherwise known as "inventory"—are cleaned, cut, and shipped in large plastic tubs from the source factory to the central manufacturing location. While this makes good economic sense for the production of industrialized food, there are obvious compromises in the quality and flavor of the finished food we eat. The difference between freshly procured vegetables, hand-chopped in your kitchen before a quick stovetop sauté, and the precut ones exposed to oxygen, machines, plastic packaging, and multiple unknown plastic-gloved hands boils down to the simple sacrifice of taste and nutrition.

Many of the so-called fresh bakeries or pastry shops in our supermarkets are not actually creating the bread or desserts at all. These are also delivered premade, ovenproofed, and par-baked to the destined commercial location only to be finished on site. If you've ever had an esteemed bakery's croissant—baked crusty and flaky outside with a moistly coiled puffed dough inside—then surely you must wonder what the heck those flying-saucer-sized, soft and dry throughout, so-called croissants that come from a commercial purveyor are. They are mere figments of their former selves.

ground zero of our health is what we eat—time to take out in!

Many of us mothers will admit that frozen pizza, chicken nuggets, and packaged mac 'n' cheese frequently are default mealtime solutions. And if the nuggets and noodles are organic, it's dinner served almost, but not quite, guilt-free. Guilt dogs us mothers like nothing else when it comes to feeding our kids. The same can't be said about college kids, though, who live on chicken (wings, not fingers), fast-food burgers, and take-out pizza too. Whether it's fingers, wings, or nuggets, a steady diet of any of these is no way to nourish a body. Add in the average employee's office break at the java-spot-du-jour for a four-dollar calorie-rich mocha-choka-loca and a cardboard pastry and you begin to realize that for many of us, home cooking truly has been supplanted by distant food-service machines.

We've reached an imbalanced situation where we spend more money to eat inferior food out, and in the process, we not only jeopardize our health but also deprive ourselves of less expensive, tastier, and healthier home-cooked meals. And there is no healthier diet than fresh food—vegetables, fruits, whole grains, meat, poultry, and seafood—eaten in moderation.

cook what you crave

Roll up your sleeves and get into the kitchen and you can produce anything you want to eat right now! Lose the middleman who stands between you and enjoying the food you crave at home. This book shows how you can make all those dishes you enjoy eating out of the house—at home. Anything can be made better at home—tastier, healthier, more affordable—plus you get the rich rewards of sitting around a home table with family and friends in a less rushed manner—communicating, savoring, and sharing stories around your table rather than scarfing down dinner at a fast-food joint or forking it out from a white cardboard container in front of the television.

Try this experiment: Call to order in a plain pizza, and as soon as you put down the phone, make Classic Tomato Soup (page 61) and grilled cheese sandwiches. Set the timer and see which is faster. It's the same foods—bread, tomatoes, and cheese—but when it's cooked with fresh, flavorful, healthy ingredients, it can be knock-it-out-of-the-park delicious.

Shopping is half the hike to cooking. If there is something—anything—in the pantry, you can feed yourself. There's always something to cook that's at least half as good as the best takeout or twice as good as the worst (see, for example, Mac 'n' Cheese, page 194).

Even the crappiest fast food adds up to more money spent than the same amount for good homemade meals. With few exceptions (and I don't mean Jamba Juice), this is unhealthy "shortcut" food with the potential to lead to a host of ills. In order to avoid the telephone, you need to shop weekly and make sure your pantry, freezer, and fridge are well stocked. Just knowing you can do this is a revelation. That favorite pad thai (see page 196) or beef satay (see page 140) is a mere equipped-kitchen and prep-cook-job away from your lips.

This book includes recipes for the foods we've usually handed over to others to make, the ones we like to order in or take out, from ethnic spots serving Italian, Greek, Chinese, or Japanese; from old-fashioned soda fountains, street carts, and burger joints; from chicken shacks, roadhouses, grills, concession stands, and ice cream trucks. Eat them out now and then, but ease a few handmade versions into your own repertoire. Sideline the prepackaged meals from the commercial grocery shelf or freezer while you create a few of those recipes from scratch yourself, like Brined and Fried Chicken (page 170), just as Grandma did. The recipes here draw from the wealth of inspiration in the outside world and will bring it into your own cooking and eating experience at home. Connected to the stories and the sources they spring from, these dishes teach us about people and places.

So leave the sandy, bruised lettuce, sugary-sweet dressings, and preservative-laden croutons of the salad buffet behind for the salads on pages 92–113. Capture the alluring flavors of your favorite Indian restaurant with a simplified Chicken Tikka Masala (page 171) or pull a handmade sweet and tangy Lemon Icey from your own freezer (page 289). Maybe you just make your mama's meat loaf and mashed potatoes (see pages 152 and 215) or simmer a big pot of childhood chili (see page 156). But cook what you crave at home! Excavate your own taste memories and assemble that personal recipe box. Restore your food traditions and make new ones. Reclaim your home kitchen!

MAD HUNGRY MAXIMS

how and why to cook the food you crave at home

★ YOU'VE GOT TO WANT TO DO IT ★

Like any commitment, cooking regularly requires discipline and will. It has to become a priority. It is a challenge to take on, but the rewards are immeasurable. When you learn to produce a meal at home similar to one you'd buy out, it's totally satisfying. We are *not* too busy to cook! If you can carve out time to landscape your yard, decorate your home, work out at a gym, or practice an instrument, you can cook interesting, healthy food at home on a regular basis.

★ KNOW YOU WILL BE HEALTHIER WHEN YOU START COOKING FROM SCRATCH WITH GOOD, FRESH INGREDIENTS ★

I'd put the Baked Potato Poppers (page 214) up against any deep-fried fast-food potato puffs out there. And there is no calorie or cholesterol comparison between a fast-food deep-fry and a home-cooked oven-fry. Done well, crispy faux-fried food tastes delicious and is more nutritious. That's the equation I look for. The minute you start with fresh, natural ingredients, you've avoided multiple layers and steps in the processing of the food that you eat. Care about what goes into your body, as you care about what goes into your car's gas tank. This is one of the main areas of your well-being that you can control. Feed your body, mind, and soul with the thoughtful nourishment it deserves. You'll be happier and stronger.

★ SHOPPING IS HALF THE JOB OF COOKING ★

Plan and shop routinely, and you will always be able to make the food you crave. Keep your spices stocked and check them for freshness. Put the freezer, the most underutilized appliance in the kitchen, to good use: you will never run out of bread, butter, or milk. They'll sit patiently frozen until called up for fresh duty. Buy premium meats and poultry, as well as fish of known origin. Onions, garlic, and shallots are your savory saviors for flavor building—keep a full basket in a cool, dark place. Prep fresh vegetables ahead for convenient use: wash, dry, and store salad greens; trim and blanch green beans. Shop weekly, and supplement daily only as needed.

★ DON'T BITE OFF MORE THAN YOU CAN CHEW ★

A big bowl of hearty soup, like Beefy Black Bean Soup (page 73), and a simple salad make for a great lunch or dinner. Don't tackle too many recipes at once. Start simple. Choose one that engages your interest—for instance, something that you love to order when you go out, like Pulled Pork (page 165) or Malaysian-Style Mussels (page 182). Then fill out the meal with familiar sides, ones you are used to making. Even the most accomplished cooks I know stick with adding only one or two new things at a time to a routine repertoire.

★ THINK STRATEGY ★

Chunk out your time and stay one step ahead of the game. Rather than feel pressured to make dinner in thirty minutes, strategize. Doing some prep the night before or the morning of leaves less to do at dinnertime. Think down the road to a couple of meals. If you're turning your oven on to roast a chicken, roast two: one for dinner and one for sandwiches and soup the next day. Firing up the grill? Make a steak for dinner and grill the vegetables for tomorrow's pasta. Thoughtful meal planning is easier, cheaper, and more wholesome than winging it!

★ ENLIST FAMILY MEMBERS OR ROOMMATES TO TAG-TEAM TASKS ★

Engage your household in the pleasures of cooking and eating good food. First learn to cook what you love to eat and make it part of your daily routine. Next, involve the folks you live with in the process. Make it enjoyable. A shopping trip can be a learning experience for little ones—especially if they're given the opportunity to choose a favorite cereal or ice cream—and revelatory for older ones. As soon as they are old enough, give your kids tasks in the kitchen and dining room. Make these part of the family chores. Teach your family to love what they eat so much that they want to learn it themselves. When they succeed, which they will, they will want to share their food with others.

★ THERE IS PLEASURE IN GATHERING AT THE TABLE ★

Once you've gathered—whether you are two or ten—important interactions begin. The dinner table is the first place where our kids gather in a small "community" to express themselves. Around-the-table talk starts with dinner and progresses to sharing thoughts, events, and musings of the day. To listen to your dining companions is a skill needed for everything we engage in outside the home. Regard eating together as one-stop shopping for wellness. While your body is being fed, your mind and sensory awareness are too. As a regular activity, it sure beats pulling the plastic containers out of the bag (the detritus of which could build a small home in a third world village) and mindlessly chowing down in front of the television. Sure, that can feel liberating now and then—but the next time you do it, ask yourself: Who made this food? Where did it come from? What does the kitchen look like? I guarantee you will not know the answers to any of these questions!

★ LEARN FROM THE WORLD AROUND YOU ★

Identify your skills in the kitchen—what are your strengths and weaknesses? Then set out to teach yourself what you need to feel comfortable cooking. Start by equipping your kitchen with the basics, or replacing worn tools and appliances. Be on the lookout for such items in newspaper advertisements, at online stores, or on casual shopping excursions. There are deals to be had everywhere. If you aren't too swift with a knife, pick up a book or DVD, or take a class. Investigate ingredients, new and old (see the pantry sections on pages 11–27). Learn where your food comes from—not only will it be culturally interesting, but it will be empowering as well. Discover food traditions in different regions of the country, ethnic neighborhoods, and countries around the world. If you can't travel, just let your mind go: television, films, books, magazines, and newspapers offer worlds within reach.

★ HAVE FUN ★

Eating food you cook yourself will give you countless gifts in return. People love to gather around food. When you're shopping, folks at the market chat, converse, and share ideas with you. Stand in the kitchen, chopping an onion for dinner, and listen to some music—make it active meditation. Start sautéing those spices, and someone is sure to walk through and say, "Wow, that smells good. What are you making?" I have an armchair in the kitchen, where I can sit and read a newspaper or cookbook while waiting for the water to boil, and maybe enjoy a cup of tea or a glass of wine. But most of the time, it's a family member or friend who sits there and hangs out with me while I cook. Sometimes we cook together. When my extended family gets together, three generations gather in the kitchen. That is where the party is! Make the necessity of nourishing yourselves a daily privilege and pleasure.

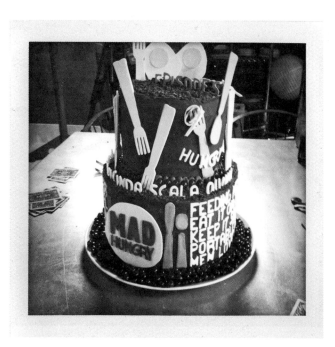

BROADEN YOUR HORIZONS

Of course, when we're traveling for work or pleasure, cooking is not an option. Make that an opportunity. Sample the regional dishes—chowder in the northeast, barbecue in the South—or ethnic specialties in neighborhoods known for their Italian, Chinese, Greek, or Latin food. There's no greater thrill for me than seeking out new foods in faraway countries. Explore an unfamiliar culture through the local foods. Watch a noodle maker hand-pull noodles, an expert pat out a homemade tortilla, a master cooking spicy chicken in a tandoor oven, or a sausage maker forming links. The experience of seeing how food is made will spark ideas for your own repertoire and engage your family in the process.

Resist the temptation to eat at chain restaurants that offer the same formula regardless of what city you're in. The allure of familiar foods, made exactly the same way every time, is undeniable, but eating them is a soulless experience. There is so much more to life! Trying new foods in a new place is a great way to expand your child's palate. Use it as inspiration for feeding your family. Expose them to new foods out in the world, then cook it healthier, cheaper, and tastier at home.

look for teachable moments

The foods eaten by family members outside your home, without coaxing or cajoling, can be a window into their untapped appetites. An unadventurous eater may surprise you with his or her choices on unfamiliar ground. My own children illustrate this phenomenon perfectly.

When he was young, my middle son, Miles, was not a fan of any types of beans. However, he couldn't get enough of the "doubles" from a Brooklyn take-out purveyor of West Indian foods. A "double" stuffs spicy chickpeas inside a soft, saucy dough wrap. Who knew?

It's hard to believe now, but my firstborn, Calder, hated burgers, and he wouldn't eat the ones I made at home. It mystified me, given that every red-blooded American meat eater loves a good burger. But Calder had to discover them himself when he went with friends to McDonald's, a place I didn't allow him to frequent. That prompted me to learn how to make a spot-on fast-food burger (thin patties, butter-toasted bun, special sauce, shredded lettuce), and he started requesting them for dinner. Now he slathers them up with mayonnaise— a condiment he wouldn't eat at home up to that point either.

My youngest, Luca, was absolutely sure he hated two things: mushrooms and shrimp. Yet he thought nothing of gobbling up a moo-shu pork pancake filled with an array of vegetables, including unfamiliar wood ear mushrooms. And the shumai dumplings he always ordered (shrimp-stuffed), although he hated shrimp.

When you do eat out or order in, everyone gets his or her own choice. Notice who orders what when they get the chance to choose for themselves; then you can begin to slip a few favorites into your own cooking repertoire. An Indian meal ordered out might include chicken tikka masala. Morph that into an Indian-themed dinner at home with a simplified version of the chicken (see page 171) and a vegetable biryani (see page 203). Add some yogurt, store-bought naan bread, and grocery-store mango chutney for an authentic experience easily assembled at home.

If your child gets a muffin when you get your coffee to go from the local coffee shop, make a better one at home for a grab-and-go breakfast—for example, a Date Walnut Muffin (page 48). Observe the masterly ways vegetables are employed in delicious restaurant items. For some reason, spinach isn't as feared by kids if it's tucked into the flaky layers of phyllo dough (see page 87). Fried chicken (see page

170) keeping company with collard greens (see page 225) seems a lot more appetizing than when just plopped onto a dinner plate with no contextual partner.

But I've said it before and I'll say it again: one dinner for everyone. No exceptions. If you haven't had such a policy before, your family will probably object. Try to incorporate each person's favorites throughout the week and emphasize the fairness of this approach. For instance, when I was growing up, creamy pork tenderloin was my brother's favorite, not mine. I ate it, knowing my beloved meat loaf night was coming up soon. Just know that it is impossible to please everyone, every time.

THE LARDER

if you stock it, you will make it

If you love to eat food from any corner of the globe, it's helpful to think of the array of dishes in this book as drawn from the supply cabinet of four basic pantries: American, Asian, Mediterranean, and Latin. If you keep yourself well supplied with the ingredients commonly used in those cuisines, the likelihood of jumping into the kitchen to cook a favorite food you crave—rather than taking out or ordering in—is much greater. Keep a running list taped on the inside of a cabinet, adding to it as items need to be replaced.

This is especially true if you live in a location where specialty grocery items are hard to come by. Nowadays online ordering makes virtually anything available at your fingertips—as long as you plan ahead. Even the multitude of ethnic shops in New York City, where I live, counts for nothing if I haven't stocked the pantry to cook my favorite foods when I have a hankering for them: if the cupboard is bare, I'm still a grocery trip away from my meal. Cooking and shopping are two entirely different activities, yet the former is dependent on the latter. If you have to shop every time you want to cook, the experience is a much more lengthy and exhausting one. However, most of the recipes in this book do not require anything too esoteric. And frequently one ingredient can be subbed for another. For example, fish sauce, which brings a particular savory saltiness to a dish, can often be replaced by soy sauce. It mightn't be the perfect choice, but it will do the job.

When you're trying to put a couple of dishes together to create a menu, peruse all your recipes first and get organized before cooking. Gang up the tasks from all the recipes to economize on time. It may seem obvious, but if you are making Sesame Chicken (page 174), Pork Fried Rice (page 202), and sautéed watercress (see page 227) for a Chinese meal, note that all three recipes require garlic and that the task of chopping it can be done once and the garlic can then be divided. Identify the needed cooking vessels and utensils, and gauge the timing so all the dishes come together at the same time.

This book offers basic recipes from many popular cuisines. Some are more like hybrids or derivative conglomerations—my recipes are personal memory-renditions of flavors from favorite dishes. If you find yourself becoming interested in authentic regional and ethnic cooking, there are scores of wonderful books that tackle these with a deep well of real scholarship.

One of my greatest pleasures on a weekend is to grab a favorite cookbook, new or classic, one a world away from my personal experiences. Just planning dinner takes me on a unique journey into ingredients, flavor combinations, and cooking techniques. I've spent many years with the cookbooks of Claudia Roden, Madhur Jaffrey, Diana Kennedy, Jacques Pépin, Eileen Lin-Fei Lo, and Marcella Hazan, to name just a few. These books are true educational studies, no different from a history, language, or sociology text.

We have become accustomed to taking out the foods of cuisines foreign to us largely because cooking them requires new ingredients, tools, and styles of cooking. Once you fully stock your pantry, start cooking these recipes, and economize your prep work, a whole new world of possibilities awaits you in your own home.

AMERICAN

Aromatics: Garlic, onions, and shallots. Don't take these flavor powerhouses for granted! First off, be mindful when grabbing a garlic head from the bin: Check that the cloves are snuggled together tightly. Press on the bulb to make sure it is firm to the touch. Avoid heads with protruding green sprouts. Keep both red and yellow onions on hand. Shallots are a real recipe workhorse, combining the flavor of a sweet onion with a touch of garlic's pungency.

Baking Powder Replace the can every 4 to 6 months. Nothing is worse than going to the trouble of baking something that should rise and ending up with a flat pancake.

Bread I buy two whole fresh loaves at a time. One is for same-day eating; the second loaf is an extra—I slice it in half, wrap it in plastic and foil, label and date it, and freeze. When we need it, it's defrosted and still tastes almost as good as same-day fresh. (Replenish as needed anytime you're near a great bakery.) I also keep a package of commercial sliced whole-grain in the freezer for toast and sandwiches.

Baking Soda Use it almost forever (really!), and when it's too old, transfer the box to the back of the fridge, package wide open, to suck up rank odors. If you doubt its strength, drop a pinch into some vinegar. If it bubbles, it's still active.

Broth: Canned or shelf-stable low-sodium chicken, beef, and vegetable. Commercial broth is highly convenient; unfortunately, I haven't tasted a commercial variety that I really like. I go for the organic tetra-pack boxes from Pacific Natural Foods, which are a bit more healthful at least. If you have time, however, make a batch of homemade (see page 57 for a chicken broth recipe) and freeze it in 2-cup portions.

Beans, Canned and Dried: Black-eyed peas and navy and kidney beans. I prefer dried beans for flavor and bang for your buck. A quick soak—rinse, bring to a boil in water to cover, and let stand, covered, off the heat for 1 hour—prepares dried beans for cooking. Still, canned beans are a great convenience. Try different brands. Some are good, with the beans intact; others are a mushy, salty-tasting mess. Drain and rinse before using. Watch for organic dried (but fresher) beans at farmers' markets or online.

Chocolate Chips: Best-quality semisweet. These live in my freezer for my baking needs, but I have to hide them. The boys consider a bag of chocolate chips perfectly decent snacking material.

Cocoa: Unsweetened Dutch-processed; nonalkalized unsweetened powder. The better the quality, the better the end result. Different brands have unique flavors; find your favorite one. It'll keep tightly sealed in the pantry for a good long time.

Condiments: Ketchup, mayonnaise, steak sauce, barbecue sauce, Worcestershire sauce, and sweet relish; mustard—Dijon, brown, and stone-ground. For ketchup and mayonnaise, I opt for the standard varieties. Worcestershire sauce is a cornerstone of my mom's cooking, and, hence, mine. Relish is relish unless you need the neon-green variety for a Chicago Hot Dog (page 77).

Cookies for Piecrusts: Graham crackers and vanilla wafers. Cookies ground in the food processor and some melted butter make a quick crust pressed into a pie pan. (Add pudding, chill, and top with whipped cream for a quick pie.)

Cornmeal: Yellow and white. There are too many good things made with fine-ground cornmeal not to keep it in stock: corn bread, porridge, muffins (not to mention polenta—see the entry in Mediterranean Pantry, page 23). Keep it well sealed to avoid bug infestation, or store in the freezer.

Cornstarch A great thickening alternative to flour for puddings, pies, sauces, fillings, and stews (especially when baking or cooking for a gluten-free friend). Sauces made with cornstarch are clear, not cloudy. It keeps forever.

Crackers From an old-school square salted soda cracker to a fancy biscuit, there is a quick partner for any cheese for snacking. Or top with some slow-roasted tomatoes (see page 129) for a quick "pizza" appetizer. They can also be used in poultry stuffing.

Dried Fruit: Dark and golden raisins, cranberries, apricots, and cherries. These are great additions to muffins or granola. Also use as stuffing mix-ins or as an impromptu trail mix.

Malted Milk Powder If you love making milk shakes at home, like I do, keep this on hand; see page 258 for a recipe.

Marshmallows For quick-fix desserts. And nothing beats a golden toasted one slipped between graham crackers with a piece of chocolate.

Nuts and Seeds: Walnuts, pecans, almonds, cashews, and peanuts; sesame and poppy seeds. All nuts and seeds easily go rancid and should be stored in a sealed bag or container in the refrigerator or freezer.

Oils, Vegetable Safflower and canola oils are flavorless and tolerate high heat. But I'm not a fan of canola—it smells like fish to me when it's heated. Safflower is my go-to all-purpose oil when I'm not using olive oil.

Peanut Butter: Salted natural and organic; both smooth and crunchy. I prefer natural to supermarket brands, but make sure to identify a good brand with a decent texture. My kids warn me against buying the "sand" peanut butter. Store the jar upside down in the cupboard to prevent separation and avoid laborious stirring just to make it spreadable.

Pepper: Black and white peppercorns; cayenne pepper. Buy peppercorns in bulk for a better price. Finely grind a couple of tablespoons and keep it in a small ramekin for seasoning food before cooking. Keep a pepper grinder (or two—one for black, one for white) by the stove and another on the dining table.

Flours: All-purpose white flour (preferably unbleached), whole wheat, Wondra superfine flour. Store flour properly for freshness and to avoid a weevil fest. If you use it often, keep it in a countertop canister for easy access. Superfine flour is a must for the lightest coating when dredging pieces of meat or fish and sautéing (see Fried Lake Fish, page 178).

Pickles: Dill spears, sweet bread-and-butter chips. I'm a pickle lover and eat them every which way. There's nothing like a little tangy-sweet, crunchy-cool bite to set off a burger (see pages 85–86) or grilled cheese sandwich.

Hot Sauce If you had to have only one, Tabasco would be it. However, the center of our dining table and the side of the stove hold multiple red and green hot sauce choices. You name it, we have it. Cook with it or shake a little on top of the right foods, and revel in the beautiful bottles and wonderful flavors.

Oats: Best-quality old-fashioned rolled oats (not instant). If you eat a lot of oatmeal, like my family does, keep a couple varieties on hand to switch things up. For daily eating, I spring for organic.

[Continued]

Pretzels Use as a baking mix-in, or for a quick dessert with some raisins and chocolate chips. Essential for dark chocolate and peanut butter pretzel bars (see page 283).

Rice: Long-grain white, such as Carolina. Stock rice in your pantry, and use it as a platform for anything. Leftover rice with a fried egg on top is one of our go-to breakfasts.

Sweeteners (cont.)

Other Sweeteners: Maple syrup, honey, molasses, and corn syrup. I like the flavor that honey or maple syrup brings to some dishes. Pick up local honey when traveling; it's a true souvenir of place. Ditto for maple syrup if you are in Vermont, Upstate New York, or nearby Canada—and the prices will be much more reasonable too. All-natural unsulfured molasses lends its caramel–burnt sugar flavor to sauces, baked beans, and baked goods galore. Corn syrup is just a necessary evil in some recipes (like hot fudge sauce; see page 286) when you want that silky texture.

Vinegars: Distilled white and apple cider. Aside from the obvious uses for vinaigrettes and other recipes, the acidity of vinegar makes it a secret cooking weapon. Splash a dash in your stew or soup at the end to brighten it up.

Yeast: Regular active dry. Always check the freshness date and once it is opened, keep the package tightly sealed. Store in a cool, dry place or in the refrigerator. Recipes that require yeast are dependent on its power to succeed.

Salt: Kosher salt. I use kosher salt (also known as coarse salt) for all cooking, sweet or savory. I also like to keep some chunky sea salt in a grinder and flaky salt as well, for topping a finished dish to add textural interest to every bite.

PERISHABLES

Bacon Standard operating procedure for the Quinn kitchen is 2 pounds in the fridge crisper and a backup in the freezer. Enough said!

Spices and Dried Herbs: Chili powder, sweet and hot paprika, celery seeds, poppy seeds, cinnamon, cumin, and cloves. Oxygen is the enemy of freshness here, so keep your spices well sealed and out of the light. If you don't use them often, check for freshness and pungency before adding to a dish; a sprinkling of tasteless powder will not enhance any recipe. For dried herbs such as thyme, rosemary, and oregano, see page 22.

Tomatoes: Canned or shelf-stable whole plum tomatoes. Unfortunately, the term San Marzano is used as a marketing term these days, so it's no longer an automatic guarantee of quality. Unless I can get a brand of top-quality imported San Marzano tomatoes I'm familiar with, Muir Glen organic canned plum tomatoes are my hands-down top choice. They aren't too acidic and they have a consistent slightly sweet, real tomato flavor.

Dairy

Butter Freeze extra butter too. I've got my everyday organic 4-sticks-in-a-pack unsalted butter. And whenever possible, I splurge on the yummy high-fat, creamery-made crunchy-salt-studded Vermont Butter and Cheese variety too (which I hide behind the box of the unsalted).

Eggs Always large. Here's another place where I splurge on organic, free-range, handled-with-care brands. Eggs make too many great quick breakfasts, lunches, and dinners not to buy 2 dozen on the weekly shopping trip.

Milk Buy 2 quarts and keep one in the freezer. While organic milk is my preference, BGH-free (with no bovine growth hormone) is imperative, especially for growing children.

Sweeteners

Sugar: White, light and dark brown, and confectioners'. Store a bread heel in with the brown sugar to keep it soft. If you find a rock-hard chunk in the pantry when you go to use it, microwave it for 20 to 40 seconds to revive it, and crumble.

Vanilla Extract and Vanilla Beans Make sure the bottle of extract says "pure," not "imitation." Keep the expensive beans well wrapped in plastic and then aluminum foil in the refrigerator or freezer. Split vanilla beans before using.

ASIAN

Good online sources for Asian foodstuffs include asianfoodgrocer.com and kalustyans.com.

Breads: Naan and pappadum. Naan is an Indian flatbread and pappadum is a thin, crisp Indian flatbread made from lentil flour. More and more, these are sold in large supermarkets. In a pinch, I substitute pita bread for naan.

Canned Items: Water chestnuts, bamboo shoots, lychees, mandarin oranges, and coconut milk. All of these make for quick exotic add-ins to stir-fries, salads, desserts, or drinks.

Chutneys and Pickles: Mango chutney, coriander chutney, carrot pickle. An Indian meal can be truly enlivened by a variety of store-bought condiments. Mango chutney will add a sweet and pungent contrast to a warm and spicy dish, while a pickle lends a tangy saltiness.

Fish Sauce A salty liquid made from fermented, salted fish, fish sauce is widely used in Southeast Asian cooking. Once you get over the off-putting smell—which does not translate to its taste—you'll realize what an extraordinary flavor friend it is to complement sweet, spicy, and aromatic tastes. Think of it as playing a somewhat similar flavor note as soy sauce.

Hoisin This sweet and zesty thick brown sauce, also known as Peking sauce, is used in Chinese cooking (it's the one included in your order of moo-shoo pork to spread on the pancakes) and as a table condiment. It's a great finishing sauce to perk up an Asian soup.

Mirin Made from glutinous rice, this sweet Japanese wine is used in sauces and glazes. I like it as a two-for-one ingredient in quick marinades in place of sugar and wine.

Miso Paste Miso is a thick, fermented soybean paste, salty and savory, with various flavors and color differences; white and yellow-brown miso are the most common. Stored in an airtight container, it keeps indefinitely in the fridge. Blended with boiling water, miso becomes a deeply savory vegetarian soup base. Or mix it with ponzu (see below) and brush over broiled fish to finish.

Noodles: Soba (buckwheat), rice vermicelli (also known as rice sticks), udon (wheat), and long Chinese egg noodles. Japanese and Chinese noodles generally take less time to cook than their Italian counterparts. Any Asian-style soup can be whipped up in seconds with a miso (see above) or dashi (see page 163) base, some noodles, and a little soy or hoisin for seasoning.

Kombu This edible dried kelp makes a flavorful, satisfying vegetarian soup stock. it's the basis for Dashi (page 163).

Coconut: Unsweetened, dried, shredded. I purchase this at the health food store. Once the package is open, keep it in the freezer. To toast, spread shredded coconut in a thin layer on a baking sheet and bake in a 300°F oven, stirring occasionally, until golden, about 15 minutes.

Oils: Peanut and sesame. Peanut oil is my preferred oil for stir-frying. It can be heated until very hot without smoking, and imparts a complementary flavor to Asian dishes. There are two styles of sesame oil. I use the toasted oil with a dark amber color and distinctive flavor in Asian sauces and marinades (the other kind is lighter in color and flavor). It should be kept refrigerated after opening.

Rice Wine Vinegar I use plain rice wine vinegar; be careful not to accidentally pluck the seasoned variety off the shelf.

Palm Sugar Also known as jaggery, palm sugar is made from the sap of certain palm trees. It comes in various forms, and I use the solid disks. The disks must be crushed or chopped before being added to a dish. Palm sugar brings a unique caramel-flavored sweetness to a dish and is worth seeking out, but you can substitute light brown sugar if necessary. Store in an airtight container.

Sambal Oelek Sambal, a spicy paste made with fresh red chilies, has a grainy, slightly chunky texture. It's a little more acidic than sriracha (see below). It's used in marinades or as a seasoning.

Sesame Seeds Store in the refrigerator or freezer because they will go rancid quickly. Some sesame seeds come already toasted—check the label. To toast other varieties, place the raw seeds in a skillet over medium-high heat and shake gently for a few minutes.

Panko Bread Crumbs These are packaged coarse dry bread crumbs used in Japanese cooking for coating food before frying. They come in both white and whole wheat versions. They deliver a crazy real crunch when used as a coating for oven-frying.

Spirits: Sake and Chinese cooking wine. Sake is Japanese rice wine; substitute vodka in a pinch. Shaoxing is Chinese cooking wine. If you cook a lot of Chinese food, it is worth seeking out a good brand of Shaoxing from a specialty store. Dry sherry can be substituted, although the taste will not be quite the same.

Ponzu A tart-sweet thin Japanese sauce, ponzu is made from a combination of citrus, vinegar or sake, kombu seaweed, and dried bonito fish flakes. It supplies an unusual, zesty tang to other sauces.

Soy Sauce: Dark or tamari. I don't like "lite" soy sauce, which lacks that umami punch. Dark soy sauce and Japanese tamari are thicker and more flavorful (tamari is even richer). Find a variety you like and stick with it. Avoid some of the inferior commercial versions, which will drastically alter or even ruin the flavor of a dish.

Sriracha Sauce This great hot sauce, which is smooth and spicy, is a must in our kitchen. It enhances the flavor of soups, rice, and eggs.

Rice: White and brown; long-grain, such as jasmine or basmati; short-grain; and glutinous. Rice stretches many meals and is a necessity for sopping up delicious juices from saucy foods. Just as you stock a couple of different pasta shapes, it's a good idea to keep a variety of rices on hand.

Spices: Garam masala (an Indian blend of ground spices), cumin seeds and ground cumin, coriander seeds, cayenne pepper, cinnamon sticks, black poppy seeds, cloves, bay leaves, and Chinese five-spice powder. As with any spice, keep these well sealed in your cabinet. If undertaking a large Indian meal, check the spices you have on hand before you go out shopping to ensure pungency.

[Continued]

Tamarind Used in Indian cooking and elsewhere, tamarind paste is made from the ground sour-sweet pulp of tamarind pods. Sold in cans, it adds a sour-earthy, slightly sweet note to savory sauces. You can also buy tamarind pulp (sold in brick form) and tamarind juice, which is actually the paste mixed with water and strained.

Thai Red Curry Paste Great canned or jarred Thai curry paste is now widely available to use as a convenience ingredient in Thai cooking. It's a fragrant blend of red chili, lemongrass, galangal (Thai ginger), onion, kaffir lime, coriander, and salt. The delicious result can be integrated into numerous other dishes and sauces.

Tofu Can be purchased in several densities: silken, soft, firm. I usually use firm tofu, which is well suited for stir-frying. It can be stored in the refrigerator for a couple of weeks. Prefried tofu, sold vacuum sealed, is used in Shrimp Pad Thai (page 196).

Wonton Skins Wonton skins are generally made from flour, eggs, and water, but the Japanese version, known as gyoza, leaves out the eggs. Prepackaged fresh (often in the dairy case) or frozen, they're available in many supermarkets. They come in squares or rounds about 3 inches in diameter.

PERISHABLES

Dairy Plain yogurt is often served on its own as a coolant for an Indian meal, and it is the basis of the many versions of raita, a salad-like side dish. Blended with fruit or spices, water, and ice, it makes the refreshing drink called lassi. I like the thick Greek-style yogurt myself. Use the variety (regular, low-fat, or nonfat) you prefer.

Produce

Citrus Limes are used most frequently in Asian cooking, but lemons are used in some dishes.

Fresh Ginger Buy a "hand" and keep it the fridge. (It makes a quick healthful tea too.)

Fresh Herbs Cilantro, mint, and basil. Grow your own if you can. Purchased from the market, they will last longer if rinsed, dried, rolled up in a damp towel, and stored in a plastic bag in the crisper.

Green Thai or Bird Chilies I always buy a heap of these fresh green chilies when I see them, and keep them in the crisper.

OVERLEAF, CLOCKWISE FROM LEFT: Pork Fried Rice (page 202); Stir-Fried Watercress with Garlic (page 227); Sesame Chicken (page 174).

MEDITERRANEAN

Good online sources for Mediterranean foodstuffs include daynasmarket.com and avantisavoia.com.

Anchovies: Brown and white, salt-packed, canned, or bottled in oil. Regular anchovy paste or fillets can be your true under-the-radar flavor weapon. A little bit sautéed with garlic in a tomato sauce gives it a deep, earthy bottom flavor that does not taste like fish. Or lay a few of the fancy white ones (available in specialty markets) over a salad—my mouth waters just thinking about it.

Capers: Salt-packed. I'm a purist on this one. Capers packed in vinegar taste like vinegar to me, no matter how many times I rinse them. Salt-packed, once rinsed, taste like capers! Their wonderful, unique floral-herbal note is fabulous, especially when combined with olives and anchovies.

Chickpeas: Canned and dried. Chickpeas are my favorite legume. I add whole chickpeas to salads, sauces, and soups. Ground, they are the basis for hummus and falafel (see page 90).

Dates A quick, healthy, potassium-rich snack, dates also add a great sweet note to savory dishes. Once the package is open, refrigerate them to keep fresh.

Dried Herbs: Oregano, rosemary, and marjoram. When adding dried herbs to a dish, rub them between your fingers to release the oils. If the bottles have been in the cupboard for a while, smell and taste before using.

Extra Virgin Olive Oil Because extra virgin olive oil comes from the first pressing, it is the purest variety of olive oil, with the most complete natural taste. I buy it in 3-liter cans—it's more affordable when you buy it in bulk—and fill a small cruet or clean bottle for everyday use. Store the rest in a cool, dark place. If you don't use olive oil often, buy a smaller quantity. Always taste the oil before using it—rancid olive oil will ruin a dish. I also keep a bottle of premium extra virgin olive oil in the pantry to drizzle over fresh, uncooked dishes, like vegetables and salads.

Nuts: Almonds, walnuts, and pine nuts. Keep these in the freezer so they won't go rancid. Use in desserts and other dishes, or toast to serve with drinks. Added to a salad, they bring an interesting dimension to the fresh greens.

Olives: Gaeta (small dark Italian), Niçoise, Kalamata (black Greek), and Arbequina (Spanish). Jarred or deli-fresh, a variety of olives will take you a long way, from snacks to flavoring sauces and salads.

Pasta: Long noodles (spaghetti, linguine, bucatini, and/or capellini); macaroni (penne, rigatoni, and/or fusilli); lasagna (dried and no-boil). Look for pasta imported from Italy. Keep your pantry stocked with a variety. I buy double of a couple kinds in case I need to feed a group. For more on pasta, see page 187.

Peperoncini These spicy green peppers sold pickled in jars add a zippy, crunchy, cool bite to salads or an antipasti platter. See also under Red Pepper Flakes, below.

Phyllo Dough These tissue-thin sheets of dough, used in sweet and savory preparations in Greek and Middle Eastern cooking, are usually found in the freezer section of the grocery. Some markets in such ethnic communities as Dearborn, Michigan, and Queens, New York, still make fresh phyllo dough, so check them out if you can.

Polenta: Ground yellow or white cornmeal. Polenta is another one of my strategies for stretching a meal for a group. The instant variety is precooked before being dried so that it cooks in one-quarter the time of regular polenta. You can store dry polenta for up to several months in a tightly sealed container in a cool, dark place.

Red Pepper Flakes Age affects pungency, so taste red pepper flakes before using. A good yet hard-to-find substitute is dried red peperoncini; if you are traveling in southern Italy, check out the amazing red peperoncini sold in all the markets and on the roadside. You can taste the warmth of the sun!

Stuffed Grape Leaves: Best-quality canned. These are a fantastic addition to salads, such as Greek Salad with Fried Leeks (page 107), or a Middle Eastern mezze spread.

Tahini Tahini is a thick paste made of ground sesame seeds. Thinned with water and lemon juice, it's the base for the sauce called tahina served on Middle Eastern sandwiches. And it's a major ingredient in hummus.

Tomatoes See the entry in American Pantry, page 14.

Tomato Paste Once you open a can of tomato paste, you can store the extra by dropping tablespoonfuls onto a baking sheet and freezing until hard, then transferring them to a resealable freezer bag. I must admit I do like the more convenient, though overpriced, tubes of tomato paste. Sun-dried tomato paste, available in specialty stores or online, brings a concentrated, rich flavor to recipes like Sun-Dried Tomato–Parmesan Crisps (page 130).

Vinegars: Red wine, white wine, balsamic, sherry, and champagne. There are many levels of quality and flavor, so taste different varieties and don't hesitate to splurge now and then. And if you're traveling to the Mediterrean, it's worth bringing back some local ones.

Wine Use drinking-quality white or red wine for cooking. I like to purchase a mixed case (both in styles and prices), keeping the price per bottle under $15. Get to know the shops in your area: a good wine merchant can teach you a lot.

PERISHABLES

Cheeses: Parmesan, Pecorino Romano, feta, ricotta, and mozzarella. Buy whole chunks of the hard cheeses if possible. Unless you know when or how the cheese was grated, buying pre-grated is like paying more for less flavor. Hard cheeses will keep almost indefinitely, well wrapped in the refrigerator. I keep all the wrapped wedges in the fridge in the same rectangular tub, along with a Parmesan knife to break off pieces to grate. Fresh cheeses should be eaten soon after purchase.

Citrus: Lemons and oranges. Like vinegar, a little citrus juice brightens up almost anything. The oil-rich zest brings a deeper note of the same juice flavor, a very easy way to dress up a dish.

Fresh Herbs: Mint, oregano, parsley, basil, rosemary, sage, and dill. Fresh herbs play a huge role in Mediterranean cooking. You can extend the life of more delicate fresh herbs (like parsley, dill, and mint; not the "woody" ones like rosemary, sage, and oregano). Rinse, dry, roll up in a damp towel, and store in a plastic bag in the refrigerator. Basil with its roots intact lasts longer if stored standing up in a glass of water at room temperature; the water should just cover the roots.

OVERLEAF, CLOCKWISE FROM LEFT: Lamb Chops Bathed in Greek Herbs (page 168); Spinach Phyllo Pie (page 87); Greek Salad with Fried Leeks (page 107).

LATIN

*Good online sources for Latin foodstuffs include
latinmerchant.com and mexgrocer.com.*

Beans, Canned and Dried: Black beans, pinto beans, and red beans. Many Latin meals depend on beans, a healthful and economic way to feed a group. I keep a couple of cans of each on hand, but I always prefer dried beans (see also the entry in American Pantry, page 12).

Chilies, Dried: Ancho, guajillo, and árbol. Latin cooking, especially Mexican, uses hundreds of varieties of dried chilies, which accounts for the subtle variations in sauces and dishes. Generally, dried red chilies of the same heat and texture can be used interchangeably.

Smoked Chorizo A dried, spicy Spanish pork sausage, not to be confused with its fresh cousin. Smoked chorizo will keep in your fridge almost indefinitely. A small link chopped up adds a delicious spicy-porky flavor to scrambled eggs or fried potatoes. Smoked chorizo is showcased in Queso Fundido (page 118).

Tortillas: Corn and flour. Good-quality packaged corn and flour tortillas are now widely sold in supermarkets, but there is nothing like a fresh tortilla. If you live near a Mexican community, seek out a small market that sells them.

Chipotle Chilies: Canned in adobo, and chipotle chili powder. Chipotles are smoked jalapeños most often canned in adobo sauce (a mixture of paprika, oregano, and garlic sauce). Chipotles add a smoky, earthy flavor but can overwhelm a recipe if not used sparingly.

Dried Corn Husks Dried papery corn husks from corncobs are used to wrap tamales. They last forever in the pantry, sealed in a plastic bag; just rehydrate in warm water to use.

Masa Harina This dough flour is made by grinding the dried masa (corn paste) used for tamales. I also make homemade tortillas with this. With a tortilla press and a *comal*, it's easy to make fresh tortillas.

PERISHABLES

Dairy

Cojita This dry, firm, salty cheese is used crumbled or grated.

Mexican Crema This is similar in flavor to sour cream but runnier; substitute sour cream if necessary.

Monterey Jack Cheese A good melting cheese for Latin dishes.

Queso Fresco Comes in a block and is crumbled before using. Some cooks use feta cheese as a substitute.

PRODUCE

Chilies, Fresh

Poblano chilies Really fresh poblano peppers have some heat but not too much; their herbaceous, earthy yet fresh flavor is extraordinary. Roasted and peeled, they can be sautéed with onions to top steaks. When buying, check to see that the skin is not shriveled; the fresher the chili, the easier the skins will slide off once charred.

Scotch bonnet and habañero chilies So called for their resemblance to a Scottish tam, blazingly hot fresh Scotch bonnets are used widely in Caribbean cuisine. A close relation is the lantern-shaped habañero chili. Both have a high heat level, thin flesh, and almost fruity citrus-like flavor. Use them interchangeably.

Serrano and jalapeño chilies Serranos are generally smaller and spicier than jalapeños, but I often use the two interchangeably. Jalapeños have been so overcultivated that the heat factor now varies widely among them; I always buy extra and taste before using. Some are as mild as a green bell pepper! Serranos are always spicy and powerful. When fresh chilies are called for in a recipe, pay attention to the size and buy accordingly: often one large is all you need when two regular are called for.

Limes The ubiquitous citrus in Latin cooking.

Tomatillos Sometimes called Mexican green tomatoes, tomatillos are a "savory" fruit covered with a papery husk. They are the main ingredient in Mexico's green table sauces. The flavor is tangy yet slightly sweet. Remove the husks before using and wash well.

OPPOSITE: A Mexican feast, featuring (clockwise from top) pitchers of Agua Fresca (page 254); Fake-Out Flautas (page 117) with Guacamole (page 116); tortillas; Queso Fundido (page 118); Roasted Salsa Verde (page 211); and Cheese Tamales (page 210).

break the fast first

BREAKFAST

PRECEDING SPREAD: Blueberry Granola Parfait (page 44); OPPOSITE: Blueberry Buttermilk Pancakes (page 32) with Double Pork Sausage (page 34).

blueberry buttermilk pancakes

makes 12 pancakes

There are times when all I need to be happy is a stack of golden, buttery flapjacks. Rivulets of hot, sweet maple syrup dripping off the pancakes and flooding a salty Double Pork Sausage (page 34) is my idea of heaven. Tangy buttermilk contrasts with the sweet blueberries, but you can make this recipe with whatever berries you have on hand. **PHOTO ON PAGE 30**

2 cups all-purpose flour

2 teaspoons baking powder

½ teaspoon baking soda

½ teaspoon coarse salt

¼ teaspoon ground cinnamon

1 tablespoon sugar

1 cup fresh or thawed frozen blueberries

2 cups buttermilk
(well shaken before measuring)

2 large eggs

Grated zest of 1 lemon

Vegetable oil for cooking

Unsalted butter and maple syrup for serving

1 Whisk together the flour, baking powder, baking soda, salt, cinnamon, and sugar in a large bowl until thoroughly combined. Toss the blueberries with 2 tablespoons of the dry mixture in a medium bowl and set aside (see Note). Make a well in the center of the dry mixture and add the buttermilk, eggs, and lemon zest. Whisk together the wet ingredients, gradually incorporating the dry mixture, mixing just until combined; some small lumps should remain in the batter. Fold in the blueberries. Let stand for 10 minutes.

2 Preheat a double-burner griddle or a large cast-iron skillet over medium-high heat. Brush the griddle or pan with vegetable oil and ladle ⅓ cup of the batter per pancake onto the griddle. When small bubbles appear across the surface of the pancakes and the edges lift from the griddle, flip and continue cooking until golden brown on the second side and springy to the touch, about 3 minutes total. Serve with butter and maple syrup as they are done, then continue with the rest of the batter. ∗

NOTE Dusting the berries with some of the flour mixture before folding them into the batter allows the dry floured berries to get "caught" throughout the batter, rather than collecting in the bottom of the bowl, as a handful of slick fresh berries will do. If using frozen berries, fold them in very gently at the end to avoid entirely bluish-purple-toned flapjacks.

BUTTERMILK

For most people, the buttermilk left over after using a
small quantity in a recipe ends up festering in the back
of the refrigerator. And weeks later, when you go to check
to see whether it's still good, you can't really tell, because
it's sour by nature, and so you just chuck it. Instead, plan
to put it to good use. Transform it into a Strawberry
Buttermilk Shake (page 260), or use it to coat Chicken-Fried
Steak (page 160), or do what my mom does: make soup.

NUTSHELL RECIPE: cold creamy tomato soup

For a quick, healthy, cold soup, blend equal parts buttermilk
and tomato juice. Stir in chopped scallions and fresh dill.

double pork sausage

serves 4

You cannot—repeat, cannot—go wrong with a cured-smoked pork product in a dish, but if you can find a way to double it down at the breakfast table, you've hit the flavor jackpot. I love to serve these bacon-wrapped sausages with sweet breakfast fare like Apple-Maple French Toast (page 37) or Blueberry Buttermilk Pancakes (page 32) as a super-satisfying savory, salty counterpunch.

8 pork breakfast sausages

4 slices bacon, cut crosswise in half

1 Preheat the oven to 450°F with a rack in the upper third position. Put a small baking sheet in the oven to preheat for 2 to 3 minutes.

2 Meanwhile, wrap 1 piece of bacon around the middle of each sausage. Arrange the wrapped sausages seam side down on the heated baking sheet and cook for 20 minutes, or until the sausages are cooked through and the bacon is gold and crisp on the edges. Drain on paper towels and serve. *

HOW TO PULL IT OFF

Everyone in my household needs at least 3 of these. I wrap the sausages in advance, place them on a platter, and refrigerate. When I'm ready for breakfast, I place them on the preheated baking sheet and cook. I also like that they cook in the oven while I'm making my French toast or pancakes on the stovetop.

COFFEE

Going without coffee will not make my day! When I travel and come across an interesting roaster or coffee shop, I bring home some beans as a souvenir. Otherwise, I'm good with high-quality dark roast whole beans over ground beans. I prefer French roast or Sumatran from the market or a can of Illy-brand beans. I keep the beans in the freezer.

ham and cheese strata

serves 6 to 8

I first encountered this dish as a little girl, when my mom's friend hosted a catered Thanksgiving brunch. I thought it was a fancy casserole that only a "professional" could make, which is pretty funny when I think about it now. A strata is a caterer's dream, and it's also one of the simplest dishes for a home cook when entertaining. Prep and refrigerate it uncooked the night before. Pop it in the oven just before brunch, leaving the stovetop free for other tasks.

1 tablespoon unsalted butter, at room temperature

10 large eggs

2½ cups whole milk

1 tablespoon Dijon mustard

1 teaspoon smoked paprika (pimentón) or sweet paprika

1 teaspoon coarse salt

1 loaf of Pullman or sandwich bread, cut into 1-inch squares

1 pound boiled or baked deli ham, chopped into ½-inch dice

5 scallions, thinly sliced

8 ounces sharp cheddar cheese, shredded

1 Butter a 2½- to 3-quart baking dish with the softened butter. Whisk together the eggs, milk, mustard, paprika, and salt in a large bowl.

2 Arrange half the bread in the bottom of the baking dish. Top with half the ham, scallions, and cheese. Repeat, layering the rest of the bread and then the remaining ham, scallions, and cheese, pressing them down as necessary to fit in the baking dish. Carefully pour over the egg mixture. Cover and refrigerate overnight.

3 Preheat the oven to 325°F with a rack in the middle position. Bake the strata, uncovered, for 1 hour to 1 hour 15 minutes, until puffed and lightly golden brown. Let rest for 5 minutes before serving. ∗

DECORATIVE BAKING DISHES

A recipe like this, cooked and served in the same vessel, is worthy of a handsome rectangular or oval baking dish. Beautiful hand-painted clay, colorful enamel cast-iron, or sleeker porcelain versions—all are worth investing in. I have an eclectic collection of them, accumulated over time, and I love to mix instead of match. And one of these makes a great shower or wedding gift. We don't always buy for ourselves items that end up being used over and over.

apple-maple french toast

serves 4 to 6

Along with pancakes, French toast is one of the few sugary-sweet breakfasts I brought my children up eating. This version is best when there's a slight nip in the air and apples are at their sweetest. I like to eat mine with a salty runny-yolk fried egg on the side, naturally (see Egg Evangelist, page 40).

6 large eggs

1 cup whole milk

½ teaspoon pure vanilla extract

Ground cinnamon

6 slices bread

About 3 tablespoons unsalted butter

3 apples, peeled, cored, and sliced into ⅓-inch slices

2 tablespoons water

½ cup maple syrup

1 Whisk together the eggs, milk, vanilla, and a dash of cinnamon in a 9-by-13-inch baking dish. Add the slices of bread in a single layer and turn (occasionally) until all the egg is absorbed.

2 Meanwhile, heat a large skillet over medium heat. Melt 2 tablespoons of the butter, add the apples, turning to coat with butter, and cook over medium-high heat until they start to caramelize. Add the water and cook until it has evaporated and until the apples are tender, about 4 more minutes. Add the maple syrup and another dash of cinnamon and simmer for 1 minute to combine. Remove from the heat but keep warm while you make the toast.

3 Melt the remaining 1 tablespoon butter in a large nonstick skillet over medium-high heat. (If your skillet isn't large enough, cook in batches.) Add the soaked bread and cook, turning once, until golden brown on both sides, about 4 minutes, adding more butter to the skillet if needed. Arrange the French toast on a serving plate and top with the apple-maple mixture and, if you'd like, more butter. ✶

Apples Any apple will do here. I'm a big believer in using what is on hand and not feeling pressured to have the perfect ingredient before you can cook. But if you have the choice, seek out a tart apple like Granny Smith, Cortland, or Winesap.

GOOD TO KNOW

Lost bread (a literal translation of the French *pain perdu*) is old bread that's perfect for French toast. Because it's dry and porous, it will suck up the egg mixture. You can use slices from a fresh loaf, but if you have the time, lay the slices out on a baking sheet overnight uncovered or dry it out slightly in a 250°F oven for several minutes.

asparagus and spinach frittata

serves 8

Another one-pan breakfast or brunch dish that is simple to prepare, healthy, and delicious—and this one is seasonally spring. The tangy sauce is a zippy taste counterpoint to the gentle egg-vegetable flavor. Room-temperature wedges of frittata are well suited for wrapping up to take on the go.

FRITTATA

2 tablespoons extra virgin olive oil

1 pound asparagus, ends trimmed

1½ teaspoons coarse salt

½ lemon

1 small yellow onion, finely chopped

2 garlic cloves, minced

1 pound fresh spinach, steamed and chopped, or one 10-ounce package chopped frozen spinach, thawed and drained

¼ teaspoon freshly ground black pepper

10 large eggs

1½ cups whole milk

SAUCE

1 tablespoon salt-packed capers, rinsed and chopped

¼ cup chopped fresh flat-leaf parsley

2 scallions, finely chopped

1 tablespoon extra virgin olive oil

1 tablespoon red wine vinegar

¼ teaspoon coarse salt

1 For the frittata, preheat the oven to 375°F with a rack in the middle position. Heat a 10-inch cast-iron skillet over medium-high heat. Add 1 tablespoon of the oil (see Note, page 171). When it shimmers, add the asparagus and ½ teaspoon of the salt and cook, tossing occasionally, until the asparagus is crisp-tender and brown in spots, 3 to 4 minutes. Transfer the asparagus to a plate, squeeze the juice of the lemon over it, and let cool.

2 Heat the remaining 1 tablespoon oil in the skillet over medium-high heat. When the oil shimmers, add the onions and cook, stirring occasionally, until translucent, about 3 minutes. Add the garlic, spinach, pepper, and the remaining 1 teaspoon salt and cook until the spinach is warmed through, about 1 minute.

3 Whisk the eggs and milk in a medium bowl until thoroughly combined. Pour into the skillet and cook, stirring constantly, just until the eggs begin to scramble but are still very wet. Remove from the heat.

4 Distribute the asparagus in a single layer over the eggs, pressing them gently into the eggs. Transfer to the oven and bake for 15 to 20 minutes, until the frittata is set.

5 Meanwhile, for the sauce, combine the capers, parsley, scallions, oil, vinegar, and salt in a small bowl.

6 Slice the frittata into wedges and serve with the sauce. ∗

GOOD TO KNOW

A frittata is the little black dress of egg dishes. Think of it as the canvas for any manner of adornment. Vegetables, meats, or cheeses can be combined with the eggs or layered in to suit your fancy. This basic technique starts stovetop, with beaten eggs cooked in a skillet with some oil or butter, and then transferred to the oven to cook evenly throughout and puff up the top in the process. It's equally satisfying for breakfast, lunch, dinner, or a snack, eaten hot, cool, or at room temperature.

FREEZER FRIEND

Frozen spinach is an excellent item to utilize if fresh spinach is not required. However, if using fresh spinach, clean and steam in a covered pot until collapsed (4 to 5 minutes for 1 pound). Cool, drain, and chop.

hash brown egg topper

serves 5 or 6

Eggs with runny yolks snuggled into golden potato divots are as simple and delicious as it gets: the prototypical egg combo found in your favorite breakfast joint, except you serve five (my family) or six people from one pan.

3 tablespoons unsalted butter, plus more if needed

1 medium onion, thinly sliced

½ red bell pepper, thinly sliced lengthwise and then halved

3 slices bacon (optional)

4 baked potatoes (see page 123), cubed (including skin)

Salt

Freshly ground black pepper

5 or 6 large eggs

1 Heat a 12-inch skillet over medium heat. Add the butter and let it melt. Add the onions, peppers, and bacon, if using, and cook until the bacon is cooked, 5 to 6 minutes. Add the potatoes, ½ teaspoon salt, and pepper to taste and let sit to brown on the bottom a couple of minutes; add a little more butter if needed. Reduce the heat to medium-low, flip the potatoes, and brown on the other side for 2 minutes or so.

2 Make 5 or 6 shallow holes in the potato mixture. Add a dot of butter to each hole and crack in an egg. Put a pinch of salt on each egg. Sprinkle in some water to create steam, cover, and cook for about 3 minutes, until the whites are set but the yolks are still runny. *

EGG EVANGELIST

My friend says that I've never met a food I wouldn't put an egg on—especially at breakfast. I'll fry up an egg to top almost any reheated leftovers. And it always works! I buy large eggs, not jumbo or medium, because most baking recipes specify large eggs. And, unless separating the yolk and white for baking, I keep them together: surely a study someday will alert us to the danger of egg-white-only omelets?

GOOD TO KNOW

Potato Pontification If baked potatoes are on the dinner menu, throw a few extra into the oven for the next morning. And even when they aren't, put in some extra potatoes to cook when the oven is cranked. They are a true breakfast friend. For heaven's sakes, if you're in a hurry, just leave the skin on; I often do. It's where most of the fiber is, along with extra vitamins and minerals. It can look cool too.

lumberjack breakfast sandwich

makes 2 sandwiches

My morning pregnancy craving was the lumberjack special at the corner diner. My husband, stunned as he was at the volume of this city girl's consumption, dubbed it the "jackhammer operators' special." The all-in-one plate included every type of salty breakfast meat possible, along with eggs, hash browns, and pancakes or French toast. This sandwich takes its inspiration from those days. Over the years, we've concocted all kinds of breakfast sandwiches 'cause they're so damn convenient: wrap and go. This one is for anyone who is calorie-courageous!

3 tablespoons unsalted butter

1 leftover baked potato, cubed

1 small onion, chopped

2 hero rolls, split in half

2 thin slices ham

4 slices cheese, such as cheddar, American, Muenster, or Swiss

6 large eggs

1 tablespoon milk or cream

¼ teaspoon coarse salt

Freshly ground black pepper

8 slices cooked bacon

2 cooked sausage patties or 4 cooked small breakfast links, halved

Ketchup and hot sauce, such as Tabasco

1 Preheat a toaster oven or the oven to 325°F. Heat a large skillet over medium heat. Add 1 tablespoon of the butter, the potatoes, and onions, and fry over high heat, pressing down with a spatula to create rustic, crispy hash browns, about 10 minutes. Transfer to a plate; set the skillet aside.

2 Meanwhile, spread 1 tablespoon butter over the cut sides of the tops of the rolls. Place the ham and then the cheese on the bottom half of the rolls. Arrange on a tray or baking sheet and heat in the toaster oven or oven for about 2 to 3 minutes, until the cheese is melted.

3 While the cheese is melting, whisk the eggs, milk, salt, and pepper to taste together in a bowl. Melt the remaining tablespoon of butter in the skillet. Add the eggs and scramble until just set, about 2 minutes.

4 Arrange the bacon and sausage on the melted cheese. Spoon the eggs over the bacon and sausage. Top with the hash browns. Squirt with some ketchup and hot sauce. Cover with the top half of the toasted rolls and press down gently. Cut the sandwiches in half and serve, or wrap in parchment or foil to go. *

**HOW TO
PULL
IT OFF**

Good quick breakfasts are much easier to make when you're prepared.

- When you have some extra time, cook up a whole pound of bacon, and freeze it in 3-slice packets. It will be ready in seconds after a quick blast in the microwave or in a skillet—and it sure beats a whole bacon-frying production.

- See Potato Pontification (page 40).

- Speaking of the freezer: if you're a breakfast-sandwich maker, keep bread, bagels, or rolls in the freezer. Slice or split before wrapping in plastic wrap and then foil and freezing.

- Have parchment paper and foil on hand, ready to wrap up your creations for the road.

blueberry granola parfait

makes 1 (multiply as needed)

A homemade yogurt, fruit, and granola parfait is a really tasty-smart way to start the day, with all the nutrients you need in a balanced breakfast. You can prepare this in a sealable, reusable container so it can be eaten on the go or left in your office's refrigerator. **PHOTO ON PAGES 28–29**

1 cup frozen blueberries, preferably organic

Pinch each salt, sugar, and ground cinnamon

⅔ cup Greek-style yogurt

¼ teaspoon pure vanilla extract

1 tablespoon honey

2 tablespoons store-bought granola, or homemade (recipe follows)

1 Combine the blueberries, salt, sugar, and cinnamon in a small saucepan, bring to a simmer, and cook for 2 to 3 minutes, until the sugar is dissolved and the berries are thawed. Let cool completely.

2 Mix the yogurt with the vanilla and honey. Spoon ⅓ cup of the yogurt into the bottom of a glass and smooth the top. Spoon over 1 tablespoon of the blueberry mixture and sprinkle with 1 tablespoon granola. Repeat the layering (you will have some extra sauce), and refrigerate until ready to serve. ✳

GRANOLA

More often than not, store-bought granola is a big buzz kill. The packaging can be all come-hither in its graphics and images, but when you get it home and open it, it tastes weird. That's because it's filled with ingredients that go rancid really quickly, like nuts and seeds. Homemade granola is more than worth the time it takes and it's easily tailored to your personal tastes. Plus, it makes a good dessert in a pinch.

NUTSHELL RECIPE: homemade granola

Combine 1 pound rolled oats, 1 cup shredded unsweetened coconut, a small handful of sesame seeds, and some bran or wheat germ. Add ½ cup nuts, such as slivered almonds, peanuts, or pecans, and toss. In another bowl, combine ½ cup safflower or extra virgin olive oil, ½ cup sweetener, such as honey, maple syrup, or agave, and ½ cup water. Stir the liquid mixture into the oat mixture. Spread on baking sheets and bake at 250°F for 1½ hours. Toss with a handful of dried fruit, such as raisins, dried cherries, or cranberries. Let cool. That's it. Store in an airtight container.

milk-and-cookies smoothie

serves 3

You can sell any kid on this healthy drink, although you need to sell yourself first—because it sounds like a sweet instead of a nutritious breakfast smoothie. In fact, it's amazingly good fuel for a busy day, even if you consume nothing else but this drink first thing in the morning: protein (from the peanut butter, milk, and milk ice cubes), potassium (a natural energy booster from the banana), an immune strengthener from the honey, and enough carbs from the tea biscuits to sustain you until lunchtime. Be sure to make your frozen milk cubes in advance.

1 cup whole milk

1 cup milk ice cubes

1 banana, peeled, sliced, and frozen

½ cup crushed English tea biscuits

¼ cup peanut butter

2 tablespoons honey

Combine the milk, ice cubes, banana, tea biscuits, peanut butter, and honey in a blender and puree until smooth. Serve immediately. ✳

ENGLISH TEA BISCUITS

Small and sweet, tea biscuits are a cross between a cookie and a cracker. They're nutritious and travel-friendly, easy to store and carry. My favorite brand is McVitie's "digestives," which are salty-sweet and perfect for dipping in tea or coffee. You can find them in the English or international section of your supermarket or online at www.englishteastore.com.

oatmeal raspberry smoothie

serves 2 to 4

It may seem odd to use dried oats in a smoothie, but it's a great way to enrich the drink with some healthy calories for much needed energy to start the day. And everything blends together smoothly—you won't even know the oats are there. Coconut water is another nourishing addition. I use store-bought frozen organic berries, which are picked and frozen at the peak of ripeness. Of course, you can freeze your own at the start of the season and use these "natural" frozen berries throughout the rest of the year.

1 cup ice cubes

½ cup frozen raspberries

½ cup plain low-fat yogurt

1 banana, peeled

½ cup old-fashioned rolled oats

1 tablespoon honey

1 cup coconut water
(or juice such as orange or
apple or other liquid)

Put the ice and berries in a blender, add the remaining ingredients, and whirl until completely smooth. Serve. *

CRAZY FOR COCONUT WATER

Jamaica has been a second home to me all my life. It's a place where fresh young green coconuts are hacked open at the top to make nature's own take-out drink. Coconut water is so nourishing that old-timers en route to a hospital stay stop at roadside vendors to stock up on the health-giving elixir to sustain them. These days, coconut water is the new "it" drink, sold packaged in the supermarket. It's naturally rich in electrolytes and amino acids—for Luca, my athlete son, it has even replaced Gatorade. Sometimes I use it instead of water when making oatmeal or rice. And it's in my low-fat cocktail of choice.

NUTSHELL RECIPE: diet cocktail

Combine organic vodka and coconut water over ice,
with a twist of orange rind.

date walnut muffins

makes 18 muffins

Dates impart a rich and sweet flavor, but they also help keep the muffins moist. And dates contain more potassium than bananas! Homemade muffins can be baked, cooled, wrapped individually in plastic wrap, then put in a freezer bag, and kept in the freezer. Take one out the night before to thaw and then tuck it into your briefcase or purse.

1 cup strong coffee

5 ounces (¾ cup) pitted dates

1½ cups all-purpose flour

1 cup whole wheat flour

1 tablespoon baking soda

½ teaspoon coarse salt

2 large eggs

¼ cup honey

½ cup sugar

½ cup safflower oil

1½ cups whole milk

½ cup chopped walnuts

1 Preheat the oven to 400°F with a rack in the middle position. Line eighteen muffin cups with paper liners.

2 Bring the coffee to a simmer in a small saucepan. Add the dates, remove from the heat, and let cool to room temperature. Drain the dates, discarding the coffee, and chop.

3 Whisk together the flours, baking soda, and salt in a large bowl. Whisk together the eggs, honey, sugar, oil, and milk in a medium bowl. Make a well in the dry ingredients, pour in the wet ingredients, and whisk together. Fold in the dates and walnuts; do not overmix. Spoon the batter into the muffin cups, filling them three-quarters full.

4 Bake for 15 to 18 minutes, or until the muffins are golden brown and a toothpick inserted into the center of a muffin comes out clean. Let cool for 5 minutes in the pan before removing. *

THE MATERNAL LINE

I learned how to make and use a great date puree from my mom, who learned it from her mother. Neither of them ever saw a sweet cake or biscuit they didn't think deserved a swath of this puree. Even my chocolate birthday cake had a layer spread underneath the frosting!

NUTSHELL RECIPE: date puree

Steep dates in hot coffee until soft, and puree with some of the liquid into a paste.

pet peeve

I scratch my head trying to remember exactly when garden-variety, commercial, store-bought, deli, bakery, and food-cart muffins morphed from a genteel size to a Uniroyal tire. More often than not, these giant muffins—often too sweet—are laced with berries that taste of Froot Loops and a flour product so bleached white that it disintegrates into dust when bitten into. They are so damn dry that you need to wash them down with a cup of coffee or tea, lest your mouth turn into the Sahara. Yet muffin making is just about the easiest baking project to do at home. So if muffins are your thing, for Pete's sake buy a muffin tin and make them yourself.

healthy bagel sandwich

makes 4 sandwiches

I love a good savory bagel sandwich, but sometimes a thick, crusty bagel loaded with cream cheese or dripping with melted cheese, bacon, and egg can be a little much in the morning. So try this healthier take for something lighter but equally satisfying. The yogurt cheese may seem a little intimidating, what with the use of cheesecloth and all, but it's super-easy to prep. It tastes like slightly tangier cream cheese. Note that the yogurt has to drain for at least 24 hours.

3 cups plain yogurt

½ teaspoon coarse salt

⅛ teaspoon freshly ground black pepper

1 tablespoon chopped fresh basil

4 bagels, split

1 medium tomato, sliced

½ small red onion, very thinly sliced

2 cups baby arugula

1 Line a sieve with three layers of cheesecloth and set it over a deep bowl. Spoon the yogurt into the center of the cheesecloth, gather up the corners, twisting them to tighten the cloth around the yogurt, and tie with kitchen twine. Refrigerate for at least 24 hours, and up to 3 days.

2 Scrape the yogurt cheese into a medium bowl. Stir in the salt, pepper, and basil.

3 To assemble each sandwich, spread one-quarter of the cheese onto both cut sides of the bagel. Top one side with some tomato, red onion, and arugula. Close the sandwiches and serve right away. Alternatively, wrap in parchment paper or plastic wrap and refrigerate for up to 1 hour until ready to eat. ∗

GOOD
TO
KNOW

The hardest thing about making yogurt cheese is allowing for the 24 hours needed to drain it. It's ridiculously versatile. Stir in any flavoring you like: Try a little olive oil with some combination of minced garlic, finely chopped scallions or chives, and/or other fresh herbs like parsley, dill, thyme, or oregano. Grated citrus zest or a little juice—lemon, orange, or grapefruit—is also good. Use it as a sandwich spread. Dip fresh vegetables in it. It even goes with French fries, potato chips, or toasted Indian pappadums (see page 16).

anytime
24/7

soups and sandwiches • 55

salads • 93

noshes and nibbles • 115

CHAPTER TWO

SOUPS AND SANDWICHES

PRECEDING SPREAD: Crunchy Fennel Orange Salad (page 95);
OPPOSITE: Chinese Egg Noodle Soup (page 56).

chinese egg noodle soup

serves 4

My son Miles makes many different Asian noodle soups in my kitchen. He's been influenced by working in restaurants with Korean, Chinese, Vietnamese, and Japanese cooks and traveling in Thailand. He's become so adept at preparing soup from our Asian pantry (see page 16) that we rarely order out any of these soups anymore. Feel free to add some soy sauce, fish sauce, or hoisin to jazz this one up and make it your own. **PHOTO ON PAGE 54**

Chicken Broth (recipe follows) or 8 cups store-bought chicken broth

Two 8-ounce boneless, skinless chicken breast halves

9 ounces Chinese dried egg noodles

1 pound Chinese broccoli or broccolini, sliced crosswise into 1-inch pieces

4 large poached eggs

Hot sauce, such as Sriracha (optional)

1 Bring the broth to a simmer in a 3- to 4-quart saucepan. Add the chicken and simmer gently until cooked through, about 20 minutes.

2 Meanwhile, bring a large pot of water to a boil. Salt generously, add the egg noodles, and cook until al dente, 5 to 7 minutes. Drain and divide the noodles among four soup bowls.

3 Remove the chicken from the broth and set aside to cool slightly. Bring the broth to a boil, add the broccoli, and cook until crisp-tender, 3 to 4 minutes. Using a skimmer or slotted spoon, lift out the broccoli and divide among the bowls.

4 Slice the chicken and divide among the bowls. Ladle the broth into the bowls and top each with a poached egg and some hot sauce, if desired. ∗

NUTSHELL RECIPE: **poached eggs**

Fill a medium skillet with 1 inch of water. Add a splash of vinegar, cover, and bring to a gentle boil. Break eggs one at a time into a small cup and slip each into the boiling water. Reduce the heat to a simmer and poach until the whites turn opaque and the yolks have set, 4 to 5 minutes. Using a slotted spoon, transfer the eggs to a soup bowl.

You can poach eggs 1 to 2 hours ahead: in that case, place each poached egg on a cotton-towel-lined baking sheet. Cool and cover. Just before serving, submerge in boiling water for 10 seconds to reheat. ∗

chicken broth

makes 2 quarts

Whenever I'm cutting up whole chickens at home, I reserve the back and wing tips, put them in a resealable bag in the freezer, and use my stockpile the next time I make this delicious homemade broth. To add even more nutrients, or for recipes with an Asian theme, add a 3-inch piece of ginger, sliced, and 2 spicy chili peppers with the other ingredients.

2 chicken backs, necks, and wing tips

6 chicken thighs

1 large yellow onion, quartered

4 garlic cloves, smashed and peeled

2 celery stalks, coarsely chopped

1 tablespoon coarse salt

1 Combine all the ingredients in a stockpot and add cold water to barely cover. Bring to a boil, reduce the heat, and simmer, partially covered, for 1 hour, skimming and discarding the foam as it rises to the surface. Strain the broth into another pot (the cooked chicken meat can be used in a salad). Simmer to reduce to 8 cups, which will concentrate the flavor.

2 To store, cool completely and seal in plastic freezer containers. The broth will keep in the refrigerator for up to 2 days or in the freezer for up to 6 weeks. *

Store-Bought Chicken Broth? I'd love to rant and rave about how you should only use your own homemade chicken broth because it's so easy, so good, so healthy, blah, blah, blah. But the truth is, I often get stuck at the last minute, needing it as an ingredient and with none premade in the freezer and no time to make it. Honestly, though, I haven't found a commercial variety I love. It's hard to make well for mass production. Even if premium chicken parts were affordable for large-scale broth making (which, apparently, they aren't), the broth must be reduced to lower shipping costs and then reconstituted. Using canned commercial broth is a lose-lose situation, where you have to take the best of the worst and make it work. I do keep boxes (resealable) of Pacific Natural Foods organic, free-range chicken broth in my pantry/fridge. If you live near a gourmet shop that makes its own, that's usually the best alternative to homemade that you can keep stocked in your freezer.

tortilla soup

serves 4

This is a Mexican chicken soup, and instead of noodles, there are tortilla chips scattered throughout it, which takes the soup over the top. The floating bits of once-crunchy, salty tortilla chips slowly absorb the flavor of the chicken broth as they soften. The basic bowl of good chicken broth is enhanced with the addition of some highly flavorful add-ins: avocado, lime, and cilantro. Use leftover cooked chicken or reserve the meat from the homemade broth.

6 cups Chicken Broth (page 57) or store-bought low-sodium chicken broth

2 to 3 cups cooked shredded chicken, warmed

1 avocado, halved, pitted, peeled, and thinly sliced

2 radishes, thinly sliced

Fresh cilantro leaves (from about 4 sprigs)

1 lime, cut into wedges

Tortilla chips

1 Simmer the broth over high heat for about 2 minutes, until hot.

2 Divide the hot broth among four bowls. Top each with some shredded chicken, a few slices of avocado and radish, and a few cilantro leaves. Squeeze the lime juice over the soup, add a few tortilla chips, and serve. *

DO IT YOURSELF

Tortilla chips are a must-have pantry item for snacking. Crumbled or ground up, they can be used to coat chicken breasts or top a casserole. If you have packages of corn tortillas on hand, tortilla chips are easily homemade.

NUTSHELL RECIPE: **tortilla chips**

Brush corn tortillas with safflower oil. Sprinkle with salt and slice or cut into small triangles. Spread on a baking sheet and toast in a 400°F oven for 15 to 20 minutes, until golden on the edges and crispy. Or fry them in ½ inch of safflower oil, if you are into it. Serve with Roasted Salsa Verde (page 211) or Salsa Roja (page 208). *

avgolemono

serves 6

Avgolemono is my mom's favorite soup, lemon lover that she is. Whenever I visit her, we order it from a local Greek diner/cafeteria in a town near her Massachusetts home. The silky texture is achieved by whisking the egg whites to soft peaks, then adding the yolks and lemon juice before incorporating it all into the chicken broth. The result is a creamy concoction that tastes instantly familiar, homey, and comforting.

1 tablespoon extra virgin olive oil

1 small yellow onion, finely chopped

1½ teaspoons coarse salt

1 cup long-grain white rice, rinsed and drained

Chicken Broth (page 57) or 8 cups store-bought low-sodium chicken broth

4 large eggs, separated

½ cup fresh lemon juice (from 2 lemons)

¼ teaspoon freshly ground black pepper

1 Heat a 4- to 5-quart pot over medium heat. Add the olive oil. When it shimmers, add the onions and cook until translucent, about 3 minutes. Stir in the salt and rice and cook, stirring, for 2 minutes.

2 Stir in the broth and bring to a boil. Stir once, cover, reduce the heat, and simmer until the rice is tender, 15 to 18 minutes.

3 Whisk the egg whites to soft peaks in a large bowl. Whisk in the egg yolks and lemon juice until thoroughly combined.

4 Remove the soup from the heat and slowly ladle 1 cup soup into the egg mixture, whisking constantly to temper the eggs. Add the tempered eggs and pepper to the pot, stirring to combine, and serve immediately. *

GOOD
TO
KNOW

Tempering When whisking eggs into a hot liquid or mixture, it is important to "temper" the eggs first by combining them with a little of the hot liquid, bringing both mixtures closer in temperature, to prevent the eggs from curdling or turning into scrambled eggs. Then the tempered mixture is slowly whisked into the hot liquid to thicken it smoothly.

classic tomato soup

serves 6 to 8

When I realized how damn easy it is to make homemade tomato soup, I was incredulous. Why on earth had we been eating the red-and-white cans of pink stuff all those years? Serve grilled cheese sandwiches on the side for dipping, or cut into small squares to float on top. Or, better yet, double-down on the star ingredient and serve the soup with Sun-Dried Tomato–Parmesan Crisps (page 130), which were inspired by the breadsticks tucked inside the take-out bags from my local soup stand.

PHOTO ON PAGE 62

2 tablespoons extra virgin olive oil

2 shallots, finely chopped

1 carrot, peeled and chopped

1 celery stalk, chopped

2 teaspoons coarse salt

Two 28-ounce cans whole tomatoes in juice

2 to 3 cups low-sodium chicken broth

A 3-by-1½-inch piece Parmesan rind (optional)

Garnishes: extra virgin olive oil or butter and grated Parmesan (optional)

1 Heat a Dutch oven over medium-high heat. Add the oil (see Note, page 171). When it shimmers, add the shallots, carrots, and celery, season with the salt, and sauté until soft and golden, 6 to 8 minutes.

2 Add the tomatoes, 2 cups of the chicken broth, and Parmesan rind, if using, bring to a simmer, and cook, partially covered, stirring occasionally, for 45 minutes, until the soup has thickened slightly. Remove and discard the Parmesan rind.

3 Transfer the soup to a blender, working in batches, and puree. Reheat the soup, if necessary. Add more chicken broth if needed for the desired consistency.

4 Divide among bowls and garnish each with a drizzle of olive oil or a small pat of butter and grated Parmesan, if desired. *

TOMATO SOUP

Tomato is one of those soups that can be so good done well, and absolutely disgusto if done wrong. Eating out, beware of a purple-tinged red tone (usually overly acidic), little brown bits (bitter dried herbs), or chunks of tomatoes with core still attached. • Made well in classic American style, tomato soup is a smooth puree. The consistency should resemble heavy cream, and the soup should be slightly pink-tinged (not from the addition of cream, but from the emulsification when the tomatoes, aromatics, and stock are blended) rather than reddish, and neither too salty nor sweet— elements achieved with good ingredients, especially good canned tomatoes (see page 63).

PARMESAN CHEESE

If you buy Parmesan in chunks instead of the desiccated, flavorless grated variety, you will end up with Parmesan rinds. These add a wonderful savory bottom flavor to many soups or stews. If you go through as much cheese as my family does, accumulate your rinds in a resealable plastic bag stored in the freezer.

CANNED TOMATOES

I've tried them all and can report with absolute certainty that your soup will be most delicious if made with Muir Glen organic canned peeled whole plum tomatoes, which taste tomatoey and have the perfect balance of sweetness and acidity.

NUTSHELL RECIPE: **grilled cheese sandwich**

Heat a griddle to medium heat. Place 2 slices of cheese (cheddar, Swiss, Muenster, Monterey Jack) between two slices of bread (white Pullman, sourdough, whole wheat, seven grain). Liberally spread mayonnaise (my little trick) or softened butter on the top of the bread. Place the sandwich mayo side down on the hot griddle. Spread some more mayonnaise or butter on the slice of bread facing up. Using a spatula, press down on the sandwich. Toast for 3 minutes, until golden. Flip and repeat on the other side. Slice and serve with soup. ✶

OPPOSITE: Classic Tomato Soup (page 61) with Sun-Dried Tomato–Parmesan Crisps (page 130)

croque madame

makes 2 sandwiches

This is a freakishly good crunchy hot ham and cheese sandwich taken over the top by a creamy cheese-laced béchamel sauce and a fried egg with a runny yolk on top. Hands down, it's my preferred, salivating-when-I-see-it-on-the-menu brunch choice. It's *so* not low-fat, it's a treat to indulge in once in a while. Omit the eggs and you have a Croque Monsieur.

5 tablespoons unsalted butter

1 tablespoon all-purpose flour

1 cup whole milk

¼ teaspoon coarse salt

Pinch of freshly grated nutmeg

1 cup grated Gruyère cheese

4 slices white bread

2 teaspoons Dijon mustard

3 ounces thinly sliced best-quality deli ham

2 large eggs

Freshly ground black pepper

1 Preheat the broiler with a rack in the top position. Melt 2 tablespoons of the butter in a small saucepan over high heat. Whisk in the flour and cook, whisking, until lightly golden. Add the milk and salt and whisk constantly until the sauce thickens, about 2 minutes. Remove from the heat, stir in the nutmeg, and gradually add half the cheese, stirring to combine.

2 Lay the slices of bread on a small baking sheet. Spread the mustard on 2 slices and top with the ham. Spoon half the béchamel sauce onto the remaining 2 slices and top with the remaining cheese. Close the sandwiches, with the ham and cheese facing each other inside.

3 Melt 2 tablespoons of the butter in a large skillet over medium heat. Add the sandwiches and cook, turning once, until the bread is golden brown and the cheese is melted, 3 to 4 minutes. Transfer the sandwiches back to the baking sheet, cover with the remaining béchamel sauce, and put under the broiler until bubbly, about 2 minutes.

4 Meanwhile melt the remaining tablespoon of butter in the same skillet over high heat. Fry the eggs, sunny-side up, about 2 minutes.

5 Top each sandwich with a fried egg, season with pepper, and serve immediately. *

A WHITE DELIGHT

Béchamel sauce, or creamy white sauce, is a French "mother sauce" (sounds fancier than it is) from which spring many variations and applications. Mastering how to make it lets you create many different dishes. Even when there's "nothing in the house to eat," you can usually rustle up some flour, butter, and milk along with something to fold in—like tuna, corned beef, or canned salmon—in order to fashion a casserole-type meal. Vary the flavoring by adding mustard or horseradish to the milk. Fold in a cup of shredded cheese and you have a Mornay sauce, which can be folded together with a pound of macaroni elbows for a quick mac 'n' cheese (see page 194) or layered into a lasagna (see page 192).

NUTSHELL RECIPE: béchamel sauce

Melt 2 tablespoons butter in a saucepan over high heat. If desired, add a minced shallot. Whisk in 1 tablespoon flour and a pinch of salt, and cook, stirring, until golden, about 2 minutes. Slowly whisk in 1 cup milk, stirring constantly, until boiling again, about 3 minutes. Reduce the heat and cook, stirring constantly, until thickened, about 3 more minutes. Makes 1¼ cups sauce. *

classic french dip

makes 6 sandwiches, with leftover meat

This French dip sandwich is actually three recipes in one: a braised boneless chuck roast, a jus made from the braising liquid, and the assembled sandwich. The chuck roast is braised for three hours and then shredded. It's piled on a split fresh baguette, topped with Swiss cheese, and put under the broiler. The cheese is melted. It's crunchy on the outside, soft, melty, and unctuous on the inside. The bread stays crisp but then instantly softens when dipped in the jus—impossible for any meat lover to resist.

2 tablespoons extra virgin olive oil, plus more for drizzling

One 3-pound boneless chuck roast

1 tablespoon coarse salt

½ teaspoon freshly ground black pepper

1 large yellow onion, chopped

2 medium carrots, peeled and chopped

2 celery stalks, chopped

4 garlic cloves, minced

2 tablespoons tomato paste

1 cup dry red wine

3 cups chicken broth

2 bay leaves

1 baguette

4 ounces sliced Swiss cheese

1. Preheat the oven to 350°F with a rack in the lower third position. Heat a Dutch oven over medium-high heat. Add the oil. Season the meat with the salt and pepper. When the oil shimmers, add the meat to the pot, and brown on both sides, about 8 minutes total. Transfer to a plate.

2. Add the onions, carrots, celery, and garlic to the pot and sauté until soft and golden, about 10 minutes. Stir in the tomato paste and cook for 1 minute. Add the wine and bring to a boil, scraping up the brown bits from the bottom of the pot. Boil to reduce the liquid by half.

3. Return the chuck roast to the Dutch oven, add 2 cups of the chicken broth and the bay leaves, and bring to a boil. Cover, transfer to the oven, and cook, basting a few times, until the meat is falling-apart tender, about 3 hours.

GOOD TO KNOW

It's no wonder this crazy-good sandwich gets people's attention. The braised meat is really just a delicious pot roast. Work double-duty by serving the meat with mashed potatoes (see page 215) and a vegetable side dish, then bust out a baguette the next day for the sandwich transformation. A slow-roasted seasoned cut of meat, bubbling away in the oven for hours, fills the house with an aroma that is out of this world. Everyone will want to stay home!

4 Transfer the meat to a baking dish and shred, using two forks. Strain the liquid through a fine-mesh sieve into a small saucepan, pressing on the solids to extract as much liquid as possible. Add the remaining 1 cup broth and keep warm on the stovetop until ready to serve.

5 Preheat the broiler. Slice the baguette lengthwise in half, drizzle with oil, and place on a baking sheet. Mound with the shredded meat to cover the bread, top with the Swiss cheese, and broil until the cheese is bubbly, about 2 minutes.

6 Cut the sandwich into 6 portions and serve immediately, with a bowl of jus on the side. ⋆

philly cheesesteak

makes 2 sandwiches

My Philadelphia-born friend is so devoted to her city's most famous sandwich that the first thing she did after her big fancy wedding was to head, gown and all, to her favorite local spot for a cheesesteak to end the night. On a recent visit, I comparison-shopped the cheesesteak sandwich shops. Here's my standard order: onions, whiz (i.e., Cheez Whiz), provolone, and giardiniera—the pickled vegetables perk up the whole meaty, cheesy business. Regardless of where you buy it, everything starts with the vigorous sound of chopping and flipping spatulas cutting through the frying beef a-sizzle on the flattop. Beyond that, the rest is personalized. Add the whiz? provolone? onions? peppers? hot peppers? giardiniera? You better know what you want before you step up to the counter. **PHOTO ON PAGE 70**

One 1-pound boneless beef top round steak

½ medium onion, chopped

1 tablespoon safflower oil

1 tablespoon coarse salt

¼ teaspoon freshly ground black pepper

Two 8-inch-long hero rolls

4 slices provolone cheese

1 cup Creamy Cheese Sauce (recipe follows)

Giardiniera for garnish (optional; page 72)

1 To make slicing it easier, freeze the beef for 30 minutes to firm up.

2 Preheat a double-burner griddle or two large skillets over medium-high heat. Thinly slice the meat against the grain.

3 Toss the onions in a bowl with the oil and put them on the griddle. Cook for a few minutes, stirring occasionally, until the onions become translucent. Push the onions to the back of the griddle.

4 Place the beef on the griddle and season with the salt and pepper. Cook, turning occasionally, until no pink remains. Stir the onions into the beef and chop the beef mixture into bite-size pieces with the side of a metal spatula.

5 Divide the beef and onions between the hoagie rolls. Top with the provolone and cheese sauce. Serve immediately, topped with giardiniera, if desired. ∗

HOW TO PULL IT OFF

Slicing Meat Thin Whether you're slicing top round for cheesesteaks, thinly slicing flank steak for Beef Satay (page 140), or some fillet for a stir-fry, it can be tricky to cut the meat thin enough. But if you partially freeze it, for about 30 minutes (just long enough to firm it, without freezing it through), the job becomes easy and the results accurate.

creamy cheese sauce

makes 2 cups

This creamy cheese sauce can be made ahead of time, cooled, and stored in a container with a tight-fitting lid in the refrigerator for up to a week. Reheat it, stirring occasionally, in a saucepan over low heat when ready to use.

One 12-ounce can evaporated milk

1 scant teaspoon Dijon mustard

1 pound mild yellow cheddar cheese, shredded

Bring the evaporated milk to a simmer in a medium saucepan over high heat. Reduce the heat, add the mustard, gradually add the cheese, and stir gently until the cheese is melted. Keep warm on the stovetop, stirring occasionally, until ready to serve. *

giardiniera

makes 2 quarts

This is a great pickled "vegetable" to keep in the fridge for sandwiches and salads. The recipe can be halved if desired. **PHOTO ON PAGE 71**

2½ cups white wine vinegar

2½ cups water

2 tablespoons coarse salt

2 tablespoons sugar

1 bay leaf

3 whole cloves

1 teaspoon celery seeds

2 celery stalks, peeled and sliced on the bias into 1-inch pieces

2 medium carrots, peeled and sliced on the bias into 1-inch pieces

½ head cauliflower, core removed and separated into florets

1 small yellow onion, quartered lengthwise and halved crosswise

2 serrano chilies sliced on the bias into ½-inch-wide pieces

1 Combine the vinegar, water, salt, sugar, bay leaf, cloves, and celery seeds in a large saucepan and bring to a boil. Add the remaining ingredients and return to a boil. Remove from the heat and let cool to room temperature.

2 Transfer to a container with a tight-fitting lid. The giardiniera can be stored in the refrigerator for up to 2 weeks. ∗

PRECEDING SPREAD, LEFT: Philly Cheesesteak (page 68). **RIGHT:** Giardiniera (above).

beefy black bean soup

serves 6 to 8

This is the biggest-bang-for-your-buck, whole-meal soup you can make. I marry my favorite black bean soup with a touch of rich and hearty beef barley soup (minus the barley). It was designed as a vehicle for some leftover beef and the black beans in the cupboard. For a hearty vegetarian option, see the variation.

3 tablespoons extra virgin olive oil

1 onion, chopped

2 carrots, peeled and chopped

2 celery stalks, peeled and chopped

3 garlic cloves, minced

1 green bell pepper, cored, seeded, and chopped

2 teaspoons ground cumin

¾ teaspoon paprika

½ teaspoon red pepper flakes

1 tablespoon tomato paste

2 tomatoes, chopped (about ¾ cup)

2 cups dried black beans, rinsed and picked over

1 bay leaf

4 cups canned low-sodium beef broth

One 12-ounce bottle Guinness beer

4 to 6 cups water

2 teaspoons coarse salt

2 cups shredded leftover beef

1 Heat a Dutch oven over medium-high heat. Add the olive oil. When it shimmers, add the onions and sauté, stirring for 5 minutes. Add the carrots, celery, garlic, and bell pepper and cook, stirring occasionally, until softened and beginning to caramelize, about 10 minutes.

2 Stir in the cumin, paprika, and red pepper flakes and cook, stirring for a few minutes, until fragrant. Stir in the tomato paste and cook, stirring, for 2 minutes. Add the tomatoes, beans, bay leaf, broth, beer, and 4 cups water and bring to a simmer. Reduce the heat and simmer, partially covered, until the beans are soft, 1 to 2 hours, depending on the age of the beans; add water as needed to keep a soupy consistency.

3 Stir in the salt and the beef and heat through. *

NOTE

To thicken bean soups and achieve a creamy consistency, remove a cup or two of the beans once they are cooked and soft and mash them with a large fork, then return to the pot and stir to combine.

VARIATION

vegetarian black bean soup

Substitute vegetable broth for the beef broth and omit the beef. *

BIG APPLE IN A BUN

new york city hot dog

makes 6 dogs

I can't tell you how many times my sons used to come home from school, to a delicious meal cooking in the kitchen, only to answer the question "Are you hungry?" with "Not really, I already ate." It drove me nuts until I learned to replicate the food they love from the outside in our home. Here I've put together the classic NYC hot dog, the kind you get at Gray's Papaya, which apparently my guys frequented even when their pockets were practically empty. Back then, $1.75 would get you two hot dogs and a delicious fresh fruit drink, like papaya or coconut—it's known as the recession special. Like the ubiquitous street cart New York City hot dog, mine is served on a steamed bun with a red-tinged onion relish and sauerkraut. **PHOTO ON PAGE 76**

ONION RELISH

2 tablespoons extra virgin olive oil

1 medium yellow onion, finely chopped

¼ teaspoon coarse salt

1 garlic clove, minced

1 tablespoon tomato paste

½ cup water

2 tablespoons red wine vinegar

½ teaspoon hot sauce

1 teaspoon sugar

6 all-beef hot dogs

6 hot dog buns

Spicy brown mustard

Quick Kraut
(recipe follows)

HOT DOG BUNS

Don't try to get fancy with the bun for this dog—you need a soft, doughy, garden-variety commercial one. They're meant to be merely the supporting flavor/texture player next to the starring roles of the dogs and condiments.

1 For the relish, heat a small saucepan over medium-high heat. Add the oil. When it shimmers, add the onions and salt and cook, stirring occasionally, until the onions are soft and golden brown in places, 8 to 10 minutes.

2 Add the garlic and cook for 1 minute, until fragrant. Stir in the tomato paste, water, red wine vinegar, hot sauce, and sugar and bring to a boil. Reduce the heat and simmer, stirring occasionally, until the onion relish is thick and glossy, a couple of minutes. Remove from the heat.

3 Bring 1 inch of water to a boil in a deep skillet. Add the hot dogs, reduce the heat, keeping the water at a bare simmer, and heat through, at least 8 minutes (or until ready to serve).

4 Just before serving, line a steamer basket or colander with cheesecloth and set in a pot with ½ inch of boiling water. Place the hot dog buns on the cheesecloth, cover the pot, and steam the buns for 2 minutes to warm them. (Or put the buns on a plate and microwave them for 1 minute.)

5 Put the hot dogs in the buns, top with some onion relish, spicy brown mustard, and sauerkraut, and serve immediately. ＊

quick kraut

makes 3 cups

2 tablespoons extra virgin olive oil

1 small yellow onion,
halved lengthwise and thinly
sliced crosswise

½ teaspoon coarse salt

½ head green cabbage, cored and
thinly sliced

½ cup apple cider vinegar

½ cup water

⅓ cup apple cider or apple juice

1 Heat a medium saucepan over
medium-high heat. Add the
oil. When it shimmers, add the
onions and salt and cook, stirring
occasionally, until the onions are
soft and translucent, 3 minutes.
Add the cabbage, vinegar, water,
and apple cider and stir to
combine. Bring to a boil, cover,
reduce the heat, and simmer until
the cabbage is tender, 30 to 35
minutes.

2 Let cool if not using immediately.
Transfer to a container with a
tight-fitting lid. The kraut can be
stored in the refrigerator for up to
1 month. ★

chicago hot dog

makes 4 dogs

Vendor after vendor I visited along the shores of Lake Michigan left me with no doubt as to what constitutes an original Chicago Hot Dog. I will not be accused of riffing on this one. The essentials are a Chicago red hot dog (simmer the hot dogs with a beet if you can't find these at your local store), a poppy seed bun (not easy to find), authentic neon-green relish (also not easy to find), and celery salt. And never, ever, use ketchup.

4 hot dog buns, split open

2 tablespoons unsalted butter, melted

2 teaspoons poppy seeds

4 all-beef hot dogs (see headnote)

4 dill pickle spears

1 tomato, cut into 8 wedges

About 1½ tablespoons yellow mustard

2 tablespoons sweet pickle relish

½ white onion, chopped

4 jarred peperoncini

Celery salt

1 Preheat the oven to 375°F. Bring a large pot of water to a boil.

2 Brush the outside of the buns with the butter and sprinkle with the poppy seeds. Put on a baking sheet, cut side down, and toast in the oven for 5 minutes.

3 Meanwhile, simmer the hot dogs in the pot of water to heat through, about 8 minutes.

4 Place a hot dog in each bun. Place a pickle spear on one side and 2 tomato wedges on the other of each hot dog. Squirt or drizzle the mustard in a zigzag pattern over the dogs. Spoon a dollop of relish onto each one, and scatter some of the white onion over each one. Place a peperoncini on top of each hot dog, sprinkle with celery salt, and serve. ✳

GOOD TO KNOW

There is a "weenie war" in Chicago between the main two purveyors of the famous red hot dogs: Vienna Beef vs Chicago Red Hot. Choose your weapon:

THE ORIGINAL
www.viennabeef.com
(where you can also procure the authentic condiments)

THE UPSTART
www.redhotchicago.com

OPPOSITE, FROM LEFT: Chicago Hot Dog (above); New York City Hot Dog (page 74)

chicken club

makes 1 sandwich

You can't beat the bite of golden toasted bread leading into soft avocado, creamy mayonnaise, grilled chicken, and a cool, sweet hit of tomato, all punctuated with the salty smokiness of bacon. This triple-decker number needs a toothpick pushed through it to hold the whole thing together. And do not forget the pickle.

A club sandwich always goes well with a gin and tonic. Pairing this one with Cucumber-Mint Gin and Tonic (page 252) results in a killer luncheon, an updated double-decker "club car" classic.

4 slices bacon

One 6-ounce boneless, skinless chicken breast half, butterflied

¾ teaspoon coarse salt

¼ teaspoon freshly ground black pepper

¼ teaspoon dried Italian seasoning

3 slices white bread, lightly toasted

2 tablespoons mayonnaise

½ avocado, thinly sliced

Two ¼-inch-thick slices beefsteak tomato

A few iceberg lettuce leaves, torn

2 small dill pickles

1 Cook the bacon in a 10-inch sauté pan or cast-iron skillet over medium heat until crisp, about 5 minutes. Transfer to a paper-towel-lined plate to drain; reserve 2 tablespoons of the fat in the pan.

2 Season the chicken with ½ teaspoon of the salt, ⅛ teaspoon of the pepper, and the Italian seasoning. Heat the reserved fat in the pan over medium-high heat. Add the chicken and cook, flipping once, until golden brown in places and cooked through, 3 to 4 minutes total. Transfer to a cutting board and thinly slice on the bias.

3 Lay the slices of toast side by side on a work surface and spread the mayonnaise over them. Divide the chicken between 2 slices, followed by the avocado, bacon, and tomato. Season with the remaining ¼ teaspoon salt and ⅛ teaspoon pepper. Top with the lettuce, place one bread stack on top of the other, and close the sandwich with the remaining slice of toast. Spear each pickle with a 6- to 8-inch wooden or metal skewer and secure two opposite corners of the sandwich from top to bottom with the skewers. Cut the sandwich in half on the diagonal and serve. ✴

Keep prepped chicken breasts in your freezer and, if your pantry is stocked, you'll be ready for many meals. Freeze them in one of three ways:

- **Whole boneless chicken halves**
Wrap in plastic wrap and then in foil or freezer paper. Write the contents and date on a piece of freezer tape and apply this label. Freeze. Use for Chinese Egg Noodle Soup (page 56) or Chicken Fettuccine Alfredo (page 190).

- **Butterflied boneless breasts**
Cut each breast half almost but not completely horizontally in half through the center and open like a book. Wrap individually in plastic, stack together, and wrap a whole batch in foil. Write the contents and date on a piece of freezer tape and apply this label. Freeze. Use for Chicken Club (page 78).

- **Sliced into thin strips**
Freeze plain or in a marinade. If freezing plain, wrap in individual portions in plastic wrap and foil; store marinating strips in a freezer container wrapped in foil. Write the contents and date on a piece of freezer tape and apply this label. Freeze. Use plain chicken strips for a quick stir-fry.

There are also three ways to safely thaw frozen chicken:

- **The fridge**
Thawing in the refrigerator takes the longest—1 or 2 days.

- **Cold water**
Unwrap the chicken, put it in a resealable plastic bag, and submerge in a sink full of cold water. One pound of chicken breast will take less than 1 hour to thaw this way.

- **The microwave**
Remove the aluminum foil before thawing in the microwave and plan on cooking immediately— in case any part of the chicken begins to cook as you thaw, which can leave the meat at a temperature where bacteria can grow.

banh mi

serves 4 to 6

Banh mi shops cluster together in Vietnamese neighborhoods, from small, funky specialty shops that offer affordable variations and speedy delivery to fast-food franchises, which in the Vietnamese communities of Orange County, California, are as common and commercial as burger joints. The banh mi sandwich is a quintessential representation of the French colonial presence in Indochina (Vietnam), where the French left their taste for baguettes and pâté and the Vietnamese added fresh vegetables, herbs, and lightly pickled veggies to take it into the stratosphere. This homemade version is just killer.

MARINADE	PICKLED VEGETABLES
¼ cup plus 1 tablespoon dark soy sauce	¾ cup white vinegar
2 tablespoons fish sauce	½ cup water
One 2-inch piece of ginger, peeled and minced	2 tablespoons granulated sugar
3 garlic cloves, minced	1 teaspoon coarse salt
1 large shallot, minced	1 cup julienned carrots (see Note)
2 tablespoons finely chopped palm sugar or brown sugar	1 cup julienned daikon (see Note)
2 tablespoons safflower oil	1 baguette
½ teaspoon freshly ground black pepper	⅓ cup mayonnaise
	1 teaspoon chili paste, such as sambal oelek
¾ pound pork tenderloin, cut crosswise into 1-inch-wide pieces	6 ounces store-bought pork pâté, thinly sliced
	4 ounces thinly sliced ham, such as Black Forest (sliced by the deli)
	⅓ English cucumber, cut into 8 spears
	8 cilantro sprigs
	1 jalapeño, thinly sliced

HOW TO PULL IT OFF

Production-Line Sandwich Making When I make banh mi, Cuban sandwiches, Italian pressed sandwiches, or breakfast sandwiches for a group, I start with one large loaf, split it horizontally, layer in the filling, wrap in plastic wrap, and refrigerate. It's a clever do-in-advance technique. Leaving it whole means it stays fresher longer and allows the flavors to meld—then slice into single portions when ready.

1 Combine all the marinade ingredients in a medium bowl.

2 Add the pork tenderloin, stir to coat evenly, and let marinate for 30 minutes.

3 To make the pickled vegetables, bring the vinegar, water, sugar, and salt to a boil in a small saucepan, stirring to dissolve the sugar. Add the carrots and daikon, remove from the heat, and let cool to room temperature.

4 Preheat a grill pan over high heat. Grill the pork, turning once, until an instant-read thermometer inserted into the center registers 140°F, about 4 minutes total. Remove the pork from the grill pan, let rest for 5 minutes, and thinly slice.

5 Preheat the broiler with the rack in the upper third position. Halve the baguette lengthwise. Place cut side up directly on the oven rack and broil until toasted and brown around the edges, 2 minutes. Remove from the oven.

6 Combine the mayonnaise and chili paste in a small bowl, then spread evenly across the bottom of the baguette. Top with the pâté, ham, and grilled pork. Distribute the cucumber spears, pickled vegetables, cilantro sprigs, and jalapeños evenly over the meats. Close the baguette, cut into portions, and serve. *

NOTE To cut the vegetables into julienne (thin matchstick-shaped pieces), first cut into ⅛-inch slices, then stack the slices, and cut into ⅛-inch-thick strips. Trim pieces to desired length, usually about ½ inch.

chicken chive burgers

makes 4 burgers

This burger—a healthy homage to New York City's premier fast-food joint, Shake Shack—is made from ground chicken that's spiked with chives, lemon juice, bread crumbs, and Dijon mustard to build a flavorful, juicy burger. For a completely healthy menu, add Potato Poppers (page 214; baked, not fried) and a Strawberry Buttermilk Shake (page 260; buttermilk and sorbet replace ice cream).

1½ pounds ground chicken (light and dark meat)

1 teaspoon coarse salt

¼ teaspoon freshly ground black pepper

1 teaspoon Dijon mustard

⅓ cup fresh bread crumbs

2 tablespoons fresh lemon juice

2 tablespoons chopped fresh chives

4 slices Fontina cheese (optional)

4 whole wheat hamburger buns

Optional garnishes: Sliced tomato, sliced red onion, lettuce, mayo, Dijon mustard, and/or pickles

1 Preheat an outdoor grill or a grill pan to medium-high heat. Combine the chicken, salt, pepper, mustard, bread crumbs, lemon juice, and chives in a large bowl. Form into four ½-inch-thick patties.

2 Grill the patties, flipping once, until the juices run clear (the center should register 160°F on an instant-read thermometer), 8 to 10 minutes. Top the patties with the cheese during the last minute of cooking, if using, and cover the grill or pan to melt it.

3 Meanwhile, lightly grill the cut side of the buns, if desired.

4 Serve with any or all of the garnishes. ∗

BURGER

I was never a burger eater until the retro-inspired burger joints raised the bar with better ingredients and clever combinations. One important basic idea drives the re-creation of my favorite home versions, regardless of what type of burger I'm making: the relationship between burger and bun. First, the burger patty type is determined: choose beef (and what cut or combination of cuts), chicken, salmon, or tuna; keeping in mind the patty's thickness and width, the cooking method, and the seasoning, the bun choice follows—size, texture, softness, crustiness, toastiness, and coating. Whether or not there are condiments available to adorn said burger, it should stand on its own two feet as burger and bun!

lamb burgers
with tzatziki and parsley salad

makes 8 burgers

What you expose your kids to when they're little does matter. Indelibly imprinted on my mind are memories of the street festivals in Detroit's Greektown that my parents took us to, and the delicious kebabs in pita bread. This burger manifests those taste-flavor recollections. Ground lamb makes the most flavorful and unusual burger, especially when the mix is spiced up.

2 pounds ground lamb

1 teaspoon coarse salt

¼ teaspoon freshly ground black pepper

2 teaspoons Madras curry powder

TZATZIKI SAUCE

2 cups Greek-style yogurt

1 English cucumber, peeled, halved lengthwise, seeded, and chopped

¼ cup chopped fresh mint

½ teaspoon coarse salt

1 teaspoon grated lemon zest

1 tablespoon fresh lemon juice

PARSLEY SALAD

2 medium tomatoes, chopped

1 cup packed fresh parsley leaves

½ medium red onion, thinly sliced

2 tablespoons extra virgin olive oil

8 individual pitas or 4 regular pitas, split open

1 Preheat a grill or grill pan to high heat. Combine the lamb, salt, pepper, and curry powder in a bowl. Form into 8 oblong patties, 3 inches by 2 inches. Set aside to come to room temperature.

2 Meanwhile, for the tzatziki sauce, combine the yogurt, cucumber, mint, salt, lemon zest, and juice in a medium bowl. Set aside.

3 For the parsley salad, combine the tomato, parsley, red onion, and olive oil in another medium bowl. Set aside.

4 Put the burgers on the grill or in the grill pan and cook to the desired doneness, about 2 to 3 minutes per side for medium-rare.

5 Stuff the burgers, tzatziki sauce, and parsley salad into the pitas and serve immediately. *

Curry Powder Commercial curry powders vary dramatically in flavor. Find the blend you like, buy it in small quantities, and store it, well sealed, in a cool, dry place; it should stay pungent for 9 to 12 months. Nevertheless, check it before using. Like any spice, curry powders lose freshness and flavor punch if left in the cupboard too long. Don't add flavorless powder to your recipe and expect it to taste good.

spinach phyllo pie

serves 8 to 10

Admittedly, this is neither a soup nor a sandwich—but it makes a satisfying meal anytime, which is why I've included this pie here. Plus, it made me fall in love with spinach long before I'd ever eat it on its own. This version, from the family of my Albanian friend Milot, is the easiest ever because there's no precooking of the spinach. Milot's mom makes her very own phyllo dough (which, hmm, I haven't mastered); I use packaged frozen dough with great results. **PHOTOS ON PAGES 24–25, 88, AND 106**

One 8-ounce container whipped butter

½ cup safflower oil

FILLING

3 bunches spinach, stemmed, washed, and chopped

½ small onion, chopped

1 large egg

1 cup sour cream

2 tablespoons plain yogurt

1 teaspoon coarse salt

2 tablespoons butter and oil mixture, from above

20 sheets prepared phyllo dough (see page 89), thawed if frozen

1 Preheat the oven to 400°F with a rack in the center position. Combine the butter and oil in a small saucepan and warm over low heat until the butter is melted. Stir to combine. Keep in a warm spot.

2 For the filling, combine all the ingredients in a large bowl and mix well.

3 Brush some butter-oil mixture onto a baking sheet and lay 1 sheet of phyllo on it. Brush the phyllo with the butter mixture. Layer 8 more sheets, brushing each with the butter mixture, then cover with another sheet. Spread the spinach topping evenly over the phyllo. Top the spinach with the remaining 10 sheets of phyllo, brushing the butter mixture on each one. Fold over ½ inch of the edges of the dough and press to seal.

4 Bake the spinach pie for 45 minutes, or until the top is risen and golden. Use a knife to check the bottom and make sure it is nice and crispy. Let cool for 15 to 20 minutes, then slice and serve. *

NOTE The pie can be frozen after assembly. Place directly in the oven from the freezer and bake about 10 minutes longer.

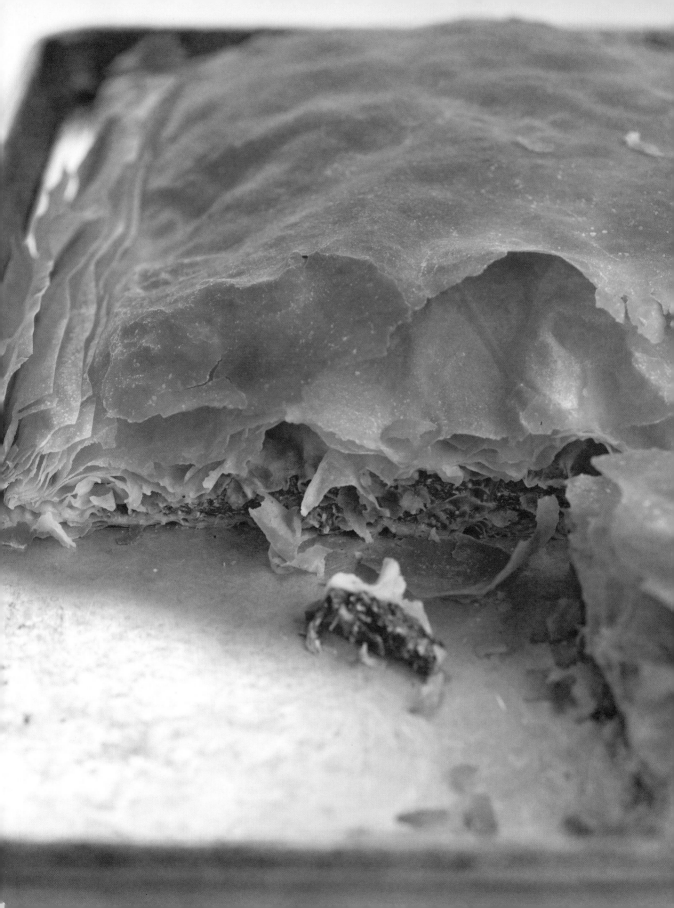

PHYLLO DOUGH

Frozen phyllo dough is the most awesome convenience item. Don't be intimidated by its seemingly delicate nature. Handled correctly from the outset, it's actually very forgiving and easy to work with. Not only is it a good low-fat alternative to regular pie dough, but it also bakes into the most gloriously beautiful flaky layers. Here are a few tips for using it, from freezer to plate.

- The dough must be thawed slowly in the refrigerator to prevent it from becoming too moist—as it would if thawed at room temperature. And if it's still slightly frozen when unwrapped, it'll crack.

- Have the filling made and ready to go before you start working with the dough. You don't want to stop and let the dough dry out.

- While working with the dough, after you unroll it, keep unused sheets covered with a damp towel.

- Use a mixture of melted butter and oil for brushing each layer of dough. This is also your glue for patching any tears: just brush a little of the mixture on the tear, patch it with a small piece of dough, and brush again. The final product will be just fine, since the dough puffs and flakes as it bakes.

- You can freeze most pies and pastries made with phyllo dough. Bake directly from the freezer.

falafel with israeli chopped salad

makes 6 to 8 sandwiches

On a recent visit to New York City, my Israeli friends swore these were better than any falafel they'd had on the streets of Tel Aviv! I think these fried patties of ground and flavored chickpeas are as close as you'll come to the savory satisfaction of meat in the vegetable world. Topped with tahini dressing and served with a simple Israeli salad, they make one of my favorite protein-filled vegetarian or vegan meals. Even my meat-mad sons and husband agree.

One 15½-ounce can chickpeas, drained and rinsed, or 1¾ cups cooked chickpeas

2 garlic cloves, smashed and peeled

1 small yellow onion, cut into 1-inch pieces

¼ cup chopped fresh parsley

2 tablespoons chopped fresh mint

½ teaspoon ground cumin

½ teaspoon ground coriander

¼ teaspoon cayenne pepper

¼ teaspoon baking soda

¾ teaspoon coarse salt

Juice of 1 lemon

1 large egg, lightly beaten

3 tablespoons sesame seeds, toasted (see page 17)

½ cup safflower oil

Israeli Chopped Salad (recipe follows)

For serving: pita bread, sliced tomatoes, thinly sliced red onion, romaine lettuce leaves, and/or tahini

1 Put half the chickpeas in a food processor and pulse a few times, until coarsely chopped. Transfer to a large bowl.

2 Add the remaining chickpeas to the processor, along with the garlic, onion, herbs, spices, baking soda, salt, and lemon juice. Pulse to a thick, chunky paste, about 30 seconds. Transfer to the bowl of chopped chickpeas. Add the egg and sesame seeds and stir to combine. Cover and chill the batter in the fridge for 30 minutes.

3 Heat a large skillet over medium heat. Add the oil. When it shimmers, drop heaping tablespoons of the batter into the skillet and gently press into 2-inch round patties. Cook, turning once, until deep golden brown on both sides, about 4 minutes total. Transfer to a paper-towel-lined plate to drain.

4 Serve the falafel with the salad as well as the pita bread, sliced tomatoes, red onion, romaine leaves, and tahini. ＊

israeli chopped salad

tops 6 to 8 sandwiches or serves 6

Top the falafal sandwiches with this salad, or serve it on its own at another meal. Israeli cucumbers, which are like the Persian variety, can be found in gourmet stores, greenmarkets, and some supermarkets. If unavailable, use Kirby cucumbers.

3 medium Kirby cucumbers or 6 small seedless Israeli cucumbers, chopped into small cubes

4 plum tomatoes, chopped into small pieces

1 cup fresh parsley leaves, chopped

½ cup fresh mint leaves, chopped

½ cup extra virgin olive oil

2 tablespoons fresh lemon juice

Coarse salt and freshly ground black pepper to taste

Combine all the ingredients in a bowl. Refrigerate for up to 8 hours. *

DRIED BEAN AND LEGUME OPTIONS

Eat them often. They are an inexpensive protein and a great source of fiber. Cooked plainly, they possess a subtle natural taste but are also a perfect benign canvas to combine with different flavor profiles. Canned, they're as convenient as it gets, but if you have the time to rehydrate the dried ones, you'll get about six times the value for the price. If you aren't accustomed to eating beans, start with chickpeas. There's just something about the shape and texture of chickpeas—also known as garbanzo beans—that makes them a friendly introduction to the wide world of beans. On Friday nights, my Italian grandma always made a chickpea-based dish she called ceci e pasta.

NUTSHELL RECIPE: ceci e pasta

Drain a 15-ounce can of chickpeas and sauté them in olive oil with 2 cloves minced garlic. Add a 15-ounce can of chicken broth along with a 28-ounce can of good-quality tomatoes, crushed. Simmer for 20 minutes. Serve over boiled macaroni shells that will capture the round seasoned beans. Top with lots of grated cheese. There'll be plenty of leftover sauce for next time. *

SALADS

OPPOSITE: Cucumber, Red Onion, and Dill Salad (page 94)

cucumber, red onion, and dill salad

serves 4

Try the cool crunchy bite of this colorful cucumber salad with Brined and Fried Chicken (page 170) for a tasty complement of flavors and textures. **PHOTO ON PAGE 92**

¼ cup white wine vinegar

2 teaspoons sugar

¼ teaspoon salt

2 English cucumbers, peeled, halved lengthwise, and sliced into half-moons

½ red onion, thinly sliced

2 tablespoons chopped fresh dill

Whisk together the vinegar, sugar, and salt in a large bowl. Add the cucumbers, red onions, and dill, and toss to combine. Cover and chill for 15 minutes (no more, or it will get watery) and serve. ⁎

GOOD
TO
KNOW

Seeding Cucumbers Regular cucumbers and even some so-called seedless ones can have a watery, fibrous inside. To remove the seeds, slice the cuke lengthwise in half. Using the tip of a teaspoon, channel out the seeds by scraping from top to bottom.

crunchy fennel orange salad

serves 4 to 6

I like to serve this refreshing salad, with its salty crunch of celery, fennel, and radishes along with orange's gentle sweet acidity, to complement main dishes of Spanish, Greek, or Italian origin. The green, red, and orange colors are a vibrant sight on the plate. This salad can be made several hours ahead of serving—cover and store in the refrigerator until mealtime. **PHOTO ON PAGES 52–53**

1 orange, peeled and suprêmed (see Note), with about ¼ cup juice

¼ cup sherry vinegar

½ cup extra virgin olive oil

¾ teaspoon coarse salt

Pinch of sugar

Pinch of cayenne pepper

1 fennel bulb, trimmed and thinly sliced crosswise

4 celery stalks, peeled and thinly sliced on the bias

1 bunch radishes (about 5), thinly sliced

Whisk together the orange juice, vinegar, olive oil, salt, sugar, and cayenne in a salad bowl. Toss in the fennel, celery, radishes, and orange segments to combine. Serve, or cover and store in the fridge until ready to serve. *

NOTE To suprême citrus, cut off the very top and bottom of the fruit. Working over a bowl to catch the juice, peel off the skin and pith. Using a sharp knife, carefully cut between the flesh and membrane of each section on both sides to remove clean, naked pieces of citrus. When complete, squeeze the membranes to release any remaining juice.

grilled simple caesar salad

serves 2 to 4

"Grilled salad" may seem like an oxymoron, but the charred flavor that a couple of minutes of grilling on a hot grill or grill pan imparts to the lettuce is anything but. I simplify the salad by drizzling the classic Caesar dressing ingredients separately over the greens at the end. Those who are squeamish about anchovies can avoid them.

2 heads romaine lettuce, trimmed and halved lengthwise

Extra virgin olive oil

Coarse salt and freshly ground black pepper

2 tablespoons fresh lemon juice

2 ounces shaved Parmesan (see Note)

2 anchovy fillets, halved (optional)

1 Preheat a grill or heat a cast-iron grill pan. Brush the cut sides of the romaine with olive oil. Sprinkle generously with salt and pepper. Grill, cut side down, until charred and blackened in a few places, about 2 minutes.

2 Transfer the lettuce to a platter. Drizzle with olive oil and the lemon juice, and scatter shaved Parmesan cheese over the top. Garnish with the anchovies, if desired. *

ROMAINE LETTUCE

Romaine is my go-to for heartiness and crunch in everyday salads. More than just a great salad green, it's firm enough to hold up to grilling and other types of cooking too.

NUTSHELL RECIPE: **romaine with leeks and dill**

Shred a couple of heads of romaine and sauté it in olive oil with 1 whole leek, washed and thinly sliced, and a few tablespoons dill over high heat for about 12 minutes. It's a great cooked side dish, much like escarole. *

NOTE To shave cheese, use a potato peeler, gliding it over a chunk of Parmesan.

italian vinaigrette

makes 2 cups

This homemade version is a fresh take on the bottled Italian dressing—and it will get your kids to eat their raw vegetables. The egg yolk adds creamy texture. It can be stored in the refrigerator in a jar with a tight-fitting lid for up to a week.

1 garlic clove, smashed and peeled

¼ cup white wine vinegar

2 tablespoons fresh lemon juice

1 large egg yolk

¼ cup grated Parmesan cheese

½ teaspoon dried Italian seasoning

½ teaspoon coarse salt

¼ teaspoon freshly ground black pepper

½ teaspoon sugar

1¼ cups safflower oil or mild extra virgin olive oil

¼ cup finely chopped red bell pepper

¼ cup finely chopped Vidalia or other onion

1 Combine the garlic, vinegar, lemon juice, egg yolk, Parmesan, Italian seasoning, salt, pepper, and sugar in a blender and blend until smooth. With the motor running on the lowest speed, slowly add the oil in a thin stream. Transfer the vinaigrette to a serving bowl and stir in the red peppers and onions.

2 Use to dress your favorite green salad or serve with crudités. *

VARIATION

crudités with italian vinaigrette

Select a variety of vegetables, such as red peppers, carrots, celery, cucumbers, fennel, and cherry tomatoes. Cut larger vegetables into bite-size pieces and arrange on a platter with the vinaigrette. *

SALAD DRESSING

I just don't like bottled salad dressings.
The flavor tastes fake, there's a weird aftertaste, and
they're calorie-laden and expensive. Some folks go to
the trouble of making a beautiful meal and setting
a nice table, but then plop down those ugly store-
bought bottles. Dressing a salad can be as simple as
drizzling a little olive oil and then sprinkling salt and
pepper over some cleaned and dried greens or as
involved as blending a few good-quality ingredients
(such as olive oil, mustard, vinegar, salt, and pepper)
together. Ounce for ounce, homemade dressing is
less costly and when made ahead and stored in the
refrigerator, as convenient as store-bought.
What is so hard about that?

iceberg and endive wedges with blue cheese vinaigrette

serves 2

This is a wonderful "grown-up" version of your classic, run-of-the-mill, bottled-blue-cheese-dressing iceberg wedge salad.

1 head iceberg lettuce, cut into wedges

3 Belgian endives, cut lengthwise into quarters, leaving the core end intact

2 ounces creamy blue cheese

¼ cup red wine vinegar

⅓ cup extra virgin olive oil

¼ teaspoon freshly ground black pepper

1 Arrange the iceberg wedges and endive on a platter.

2 Crumble the blue cheese into a jar. Using a fork, smash up the cheese a little bit. Add the vinegar, olive oil, and pepper, put the lid on the jar, and shake the dressing until combined and creamy.

3 Pour a few tablespoons of the dressing over the salad and serve. Store the extra dressing in the refrigerator for up to 2 weeks. *

ICEBERG LETTUCE

Don't be hating on iceberg, even if it's the fashionable thing to do. Yes, darker leafy greens have more nutritional value and fiber for sure, but don't discount the pleasure and mouthfeel of biting into a cool, crunchy vegetable (can I call it a vegetable?) swathed in a creamy sauce.

cobb salad

serves 6 to 8

I've never met a salad lover who doesn't love a good Cobb—especially my female friends who live on salads. It's funny how this one salad can go high or low, depending on whether you're in a Denny's or an upscale American bistro and using food-service ingredients or "farm-sourced" ones. But this recipe is ideal for personalizing when making it at home. A meal in itself, it features a different ingredient for everyone, including our favorite, bacon—a guy magnet if there ever was one.

1 head romaine lettuce, trimmed and chopped

1 head butter lettuce, cored and chopped

Two 8-ounce chicken breasts, poached (see Note) or grilled, chopped

6 slices bacon, cooked until crisp and chopped

2 medium tomatoes, chopped

4 hard-boiled eggs, quartered

1 avocado, halved, pitted, peeled, and chopped

4 ounces Roquefort cheese, crumbled

¼ cup chopped fresh chives

VINAIGRETTE

1 tablespoon Dijon mustard

¼ cup red wine vinegar

2 teaspoons Worcestershire sauce

1 garlic clove

½ teaspoon coarse salt

½ cup extra virgin olive oil

¼ teaspoon freshly ground black pepper

1 Spread the lettuce on a large rectangular platter. Working from one side of the platter to the other, arrange the remaining salad ingredients on top of the lettuce in rows, making stripes. Chill in the refrigerator for up to 2 hours until ready to serve.

2 For the vinaigrette, whisk together the mustard, vinegar, and Worcestershire sauce in a medium bowl. Mince the garlic with the salt and mash with the side of the knife until it becomes a paste. Add to the bowl, whisking constantly. Slowly pour in the olive oil in a thin stream, whisking until thick and creamy. Whisk in the pepper.

3 Pour the dressing over the salad and serve. *

Pedigree This salad hails from an old-time Los Angeles restaurant, The Brown Derby. Supposedly one night in the 1930s, its owner, Mr. Cobb, and a friend, hankering after a late-night snack, tinkered around in the kitchen with some leftovers. When the friend returned the next day, he requested the same dish—and the Cobb salad was born.

To poach chicken for salads, soups, and tacos, put 2 chicken breasts in a small saucepan, cover with chicken broth or water by 2 inches, and add one or more aromatics such as onion, garlic, carrot, celery, black peppercorns, and bay leaf. Cover and bring to a boil, then reduce heat to a simmer, and cook until just cooked through, 12 to 15 minutes (an instant-read thermometer inserted into the thickest part of the breast should register 160°F). Remove the chicken from the poaching liquid (if you used chicken broth, strain it and reserve for another use) and let rest until cool. Slice or shred the chicken to use immediately, or store whole in the refrigerator in a resealable plastic bag for up to 2 days.

HOW TO MAKE HARD-BOILED EGGS

Don't take hard-boiled eggs for granted: they can be divine little morsels of textural, buttery heaven or sulphurized, smelly turnoffs. Too many people just throw the eggs into boiling water and cook until rubberized. Here is my favorite method, after much trial and error.

NUTSHELL RECIPE: **hard-boiled eggs**

Put the (large) eggs in a pot and cover with cold water. Bring to a boil; don't walk away and let them boil away unnoticed. Remove the pan from the heat, cover, and let sit for 10 minutes. Drain and submerge in cold water to cool before peeling. The yolks will be just barely cooked and the whites fully cooked, tender, and without bounce. ★

beet, carrot, and watercress salad

serves 4 to 6

I'm crazy about this salad, created by my son Miles. Having worked in a restaurant kitchen, he effort-lessly applies professional cooking techniques to any dish he makes. Here the beets and carrots are cooked separately and slightly differently, to accentuate their flavors. The sweetness of the carrots is enhanced by cooking them with sugar; vinegar tempers the beets with its acidic tang. The radishes bring a crunchy pungency. Chilling the cooked vegetables before assembling enhances the differ-ences. The peppery watercress complements everything. Finished with a drizzle of olive oil and a sprinkling of salt and pepper, the salad has a wonderfully balanced mix of sweet, salty, and acidic.

4 medium beets

½ cup sherry vinegar

Coarse salt

1 tablespoon safflower oil

4 small carrots, peeled and cut ¼ inch thick on the bias

2 tablespoons sugar

1 bunch watercress, washed and dried, thick stems removed

3 radishes, thinly sliced

Freshly ground black pepper

Extra virgin olive oil

1 Put the beets in a medium saucepan with the vinegar, a large pinch of salt, and water to cover. Cover the pan with aluminum foil and poke 4 holes in the foil. Cook until the beets are tender (a knife should easily pierce one), about 45 minutes. Allow the beets to cool, then drain and cut each into 8 wedges. Chill in the refrigerator.

2 Meanwhile, heat a medium sauté pan over medium-high heat, then add the vegetable oil and carrots, and cook until golden brown on the first side. Add the sugar, stir, and cook until the carrots are tender and crispy, 5 to 7 minutes. Allow the carrots to cool, then chill in the refrigerator.

3 Put the watercress in a salad bowl. Add the radishes, beets, and carrots and season with salt and pepper. Toss, drizzle with olive oil, and serve. *

WATERCRESS

Do not overlook this power vegetable—it's not just a pretty garnish. Each crunchy, peppery bite is loaded with phytonutrients and antioxidants, powered by iron, calcium, and folic acid. And it's another green vegetable usually eaten fresh that also loves to be cooked; see Stir-Fried Watercress with Garlic (page 227).

greek salad with fried leeks

serves 4 to 6

Many iterations of this salad exist, from the basic Greek-diner type to more upscale versions. I love its simplicity and the juxtaposition of the vegetables, cheese, olives, and stuffed grape leaves. The addition of fried shredded leeks had me returning weekly to my neighborhood restaurant where I discovered the idea. I serve it with Spinach Phyllo Pie (page 87) for a satisfying vegetarian meal.

1½ cups safflower oil

1 leek, white and pale green parts only, washed well, cut into 3-inch-long julienne (see Note, page 83)

One 15½-ounce can chickpeas, drained, rinsed, and patted dry

1 tablespoon red wine vinegar

½ teaspoon coarse salt

¼ teaspoon freshly ground black pepper

1 tablespoon extra virgin olive oil

1 English cucumber, peeled, quartered lengthwise, and sliced ⅓ inch thick

1 pint grape tomatoes, halved

½ cup Kalamata olives, pitted and halved

1 romaine heart, trimmed and sliced ½ inch thick

6 ounces store-bought stuffed grape leaves, quartered crosswise

4 ounces Greek feta cheese, crumbled

1. Heat an 8-inch skillet over medium-high heat. Add the safflower oil (see Note, page 171). Once it shimmers, working in 2 or 3 batches, add the leeks and fry until golden brown, about 2 minutes. Transfer to a paper-towel-lined plate.

2. Fry the chickpeas in 2 batches until golden brown, about 2 minutes per batch. Transfer to a paper-towel-lined plate.

3. Whisk together the vinegar, salt, pepper, and oil in a medium bowl. Add the cucumber, tomatoes, and olives and toss to combine.

4. Spread the romaine on a large platter and cover with the dressed vegetables. Top with the grape leaves, chickpeas, leeks, and feta and serve. ∗

CHICKPEAS

I love chickpeas plain in Greek salads, but fried chickpeas offer a whole new texture to enjoy. Also try them seasoned and fried to serve as a bar snack with drinks.

NUTSHELL RECIPE: **spiced chickpea snack**

Rinse and dry canned chickpeas and toss with olive oil, salt, pepper, and a favorite spice like cumin or garam masala (see page 17). Spread on a baking sheet and roast in a 400°F oven for 20 minutes, until golden and slightly firm. ∗

OPPOSITE: Greek Salad with Fried Leeks (above) and Spinach Phyllo Pie (page 87)

burger salad

serves 2

One night, when I got home from work, there was "nothing in the house to eat" (a common complaint from my children). My husband pulled a burger from the freezer and the last vegetable and a few lonely scallions from the crisper, and made the most satisfying and delicious warm salad.

Wow, a burger in a salad? Hells yeah! Now I purposely shop for the ingredients for this dinner.

6 ounces ground beef

Coarse salt and freshly ground black pepper

Dash of Worcestershire sauce or soy sauce

1 small head broccoli, separated into large florets, stalk peeled and thinly sliced

Extra virgin olive oil for drizzling

2 scallions, thinly sliced

Hot sauce, such as Sriracha

1 Heat a cast-iron skillet over medium-high heat until hot. Shape the beef into 2 patties that are ½ inch thick and season with salt and pepper. Cook for 3 to 4 minutes, until slightly charred. Flip the burgers and continue cooking. After 2 minutes, add a splash of Worcestershire sauce and swirl it in the pan for about 30 seconds to deglaze. Turn the burgers again just to coat with the glaze and remove from the heat.

2 Meanwhile, steam the broccoli until just tender, about 5 minutes.

3 Toss the broccoli with a drizzle of olive oil in a large bowl. Chop or crumble the burgers into the broccoli. Sprinkle with the scallions. Sprinkle on some hot sauce. Toss everything together and serve. ∗

FREEZER FRIEND

This salad can, literally, be pulled from the freezer. If you buy ground beef, form it into patties, wrap individually, and stick in the freezer, you're always ready for a burger—or burger salad! (I've even pulled out a couple of patties to crumble and cook with tomato sauce for a desperation pasta meal.) And, believe it or not, frozen broccoli florets are perfectly acceptable in a pinch. Broccoli is one of the few vegetables—along with corn, and spinach, and peas—that I keep stocked for emergencies.

sausage and pepper salad
with golden crostini

serves 5

"Sauseege and pippeez" is our street fair favorite. The scent wafting from the vendor carts conjures up memories of my grandmother's Italian kitchen. Updated for a new generation, here the sausages and vegetables are perched atop lettuce and licoricey fennel rather than tucked into fat, doughy rolls. Ciabatta bread is sliced and toasted for a crispy crouton-like contrast to the salad.

2 hot Italian sausages, removed from casings

4 sweet Italian sausages, removed from casings

1 yellow bell pepper, cored, seeded, and cut into ½-inch-wide strips

1 large shallot or 2 small shallots, thinly sliced

¼ cup dry white wine

2 tablespoons extra virgin olive oil

4 garlic cloves, smashed and peeled

5 slices ciabatta or rustic white Italian bread

1 head romaine lettuce, trimmed and cut into 1½-inch pieces

1 small fennel bulb, trimmed and very thinly sliced

1 tablespoon white wine vinegar

Coarse salt and freshly ground black pepper

¼ cup shaved Parmesan cheese

Out-of-the-Casing Sausage Sausages can be a convenience food. Slice the links open and remove the meat from the casing. Already seasoned and ready, it's a simple, delicious base for a meat sauce (see page 150). Or crumble and cook to layer it into lasagna.

1 Put the sausage in a large skillet and sauté, using a metal spatula to break up the pieces, until golden brown with some crispy bits, about 10 minutes. Transfer to a paper-towel-lined plate.

2 Add the peppers and shallots to the pan and sauté until softened, about 5 minutes. Add the wine, stirring to deglaze the pan (see Note) and cook to reduce it to a slight glaze coating the peppers. Place the pepper mixture on top of the sausage.

3 Add 1 tablespoon of the olive oil and the garlic to the pan and let the garlic sizzle; remove before it turns brown. Add the bread and cook until golden on the first side, about 2 minutes. Drizzle the remaining tablespoon of olive oil over the bread, turn, and continue cooking until crisp. Remove from the heat.

4 Toss the lettuce and fennel in a large bowl, then add the sausage and pepper mixture. Drizzle the vinegar over, sprinkle with salt and a generous grind of black pepper, and toss well. Serve in large salad bowls, topped with the shaved Parmesan and crostini. ∗

NOTE Deglazing is a technique where a liquid (such as broth, wine, or vinegar) is used to dislodge the yummy caramelized bits that adhere to the bottom of a pan during cooking. Add the liquid when the heat is high. Using a wooden spoon or spatula, scrape the flavor nuggets off the bottom of the pan and stir into the liquid as it reduces and concentrates in flavor.

corn salad

serves 6 to 8

This has always been a staple in my mother's house during the summer, when corn is sweet and tomatoes are at their peak. Vary the herbs and acid to your taste, subbing in cilantro, mint, or dill and lemon juice, orange juice, or rice wine vinegar.

6 ears corn	**1** Strip the corn from the cobs into a large bowl. With the edge of a spoon, scrape the corn "milk" (see Note) from the cobs into the bowl. Add the remaining ingredients and stir to combine.
2 medium tomatoes, chopped	
3 scallions, thinly sliced	
¼ cup thinly sliced fresh basil leaves	
Juice of 1 lime	**2** The salad can be made a day ahead and stored in the fridge. Remove from the refrigerator at least 30 minutes before serving. ＊
¼ cup extra virgin olive oil	
½ teaspoon coarse salt	
¼ teaspoon freshly ground black pepper	

NOTE Corn milk is the liquid released from the raw kernels when they are cut off the cob. Once the kernels are removed, some milk still remains on the cob. Don't waste it, since it contains a sweet corny essence that intensifies the flavor of this salad.

HOW TO PULL IT OFF Stripping corn from the cob can be awkward. I see folks slicing down between kernels and cob inside a bowl to catch all the flying kernels, but I find it difficult to get a good grip on the corn unless the cob is on a flat surface. And a 10-inch cob can be hard to hold and slice while using a sharp knife. So, after I shuck the corn and remove all the silk, I break the cobs in half so each piece is about 4 or 5 inches long. These are much easier to hold upright on a counter or cutting board and shave. Bring on the flying kernels.

OPPOSITE: Corn Salad (above) and Escarole and Date Salad with Parmesan (page 112)

escarole and date salad with parmesan

serves 6

Adding an unexpected ingredient like dates can give a favorite salad recipe a whole new flavor dimension. Bitter escarole and radicchio, salty Parmesan, and sweet, chewy dates combine in a contrasting taste explosion. Use half a head of escarole for this salad and store the rest in a resealable bag in the fridge for later use. **PHOTO ON PAGE 110**

½ head escarole, trimmed, sliced lengthwise in half, and thinly sliced crosswise

1 head radicchio, cored and thinly sliced

⅓ cup thinly sliced pitted dates

⅓ cup fresh lemon juice

½ teaspoon Dijon mustard

¼ cup grated Parmesan, plus shavings for optional garnish

½ cup extra virgin olive oil

Freshly ground black pepper

1 Combine the escarole and radicchio in a large salad bowl. Toss in the dates.

2 Combine the lemon juice, mustard, grated Parmesan, olive oil, and black pepper to taste in a jar with a tight-fitting lid and shake well to combine. Pour over the salad and toss. Serve with shaved Parmesan, if desired. *

ESCAROLE

One thing I preach is greens, greens, and more greens; we eat them most nights at home, fresh or cooked. Escarole is an often-overlooked player, but growing up with an Italian heritage, I got it sautéed with olive oil and garlic, floating in a meatball soup, and layered or stuffed into macaroni. Fresh, it has an aggressive flavor and texture, making it ideal paired with anchovies—dare I say—or contrasted with a sweet ingredient, as it is in this salad. When using a firm-textured, bitter green like this, tear or cut the leaves into bite-size pieces so it's easier to chew.

modern ambrosia fruit salad

serves 4

I love the cool, sweet contrast of fruit to cream in this retro 1950s fruit salad, but not the typical commercial recipe ingredients—fake-cream Cool Whip and marshmallows. So I've modernized and cleaned it up it with honey-sweetened yogurt and the addition of kiwis.

3 mandarin oranges, peeled, sectioned, and sections cut crosswise in half, or 1 cup canned mandarin oranges (see below)

½ pineapple, peeled, cored, and cut into ¾-inch chunks (2 cups)

3 kiwis, peeled, quartered lengthwise, and sliced crosswise (1 cup)

1 cup sweetened flaked coconut, plus some for garnish

1 cup Greek-style yogurt

1 tablespoon honey

½ teaspoon pure vanilla extract

1. Put the oranges, pineapple, kiwi, and coconut in a serving bowl and toss to combine.

2. Whisk together the yogurt, honey, and vanilla. Fold into the fruit, garnish with coconut, and serve. *

MANDARIN ORANGES

Mandarins are a beautiful little fruit with a unique and different citrus flavor. But since fresh ones are not often available, even in season, I keep a few cans in the pantry. They're great for a quick salad add-in or dessert—they will help you if you let them. For instance, in Orange Creamsicle Float (page 257), they are muddled before the ice cream and some soda are added, for a quick and satisfying sweet. Or serve with canned lychees and fortune cookies to complete a Chinese feast, or with squares of bittersweet chocolate and toasted nuts for a snack.

CHAPTER FOUR

NOSHES AND NIBBLES

OPPOSITE: Guacamole (page 116) and Fake-Out Flautas (page 117)

guacamole

makes 2 cups

Store-bought guacamole mystifies me. Why buy something that simply requires mashing up a few items? And the homemade version is so much better. There are many riffs on guacamole these days, with various vegetables, fruits, or smoked chorizo added to personalize and differentiate them. But my old-school preference is for this version: it was the first Mexican recipe I learned. My early training in Mexican cooking came from Diana Kennedy, an absolute purist author-teacher of authentic regional Mexican food. **PHOTO ON PAGE 114**

¼ cup finely chopped white onion

2 serrano chilies, minced (about 2 tablespoons)

3 tablespoons chopped fresh cilantro

1 teaspoon coarse salt

3 ripe Hass avocados, halved, pitted, and flesh scooped out of skin

1 small tomato, chopped

Tortilla chips, warm tortillas, or flautas (opposite) for serving

1 Mix together the onion, chilies, 2 tablespoons of the cilantro, and the salt in a large bowl. Using a large fork, crush the avocados into the onion mixture, leaving the mixture somewhat chunky. Fold in the tomatoes. Sprinkle the remaining tablespoon of cilantro over the mixture.

2 Serve with tortilla chips, warm tortillas, or flautas. ✳

AVOCADOS

Perfectly ripe avocados are the key to this recipe, so you will probably have to plan ahead. Either find where to buy avocados that are cared for by a produce manager who knows how to keep ripe ones at the ready, or buy them in advance and let them ripen on your counter. Put the avocados in a paper bag or wrap in newspaper to mature—a process that will be hastened by snuggling an apple or tomato next to them. Check them every day, and don't let them get overripe.

fake-out flautas

makes 12 flautas; serves 6

When I first made these at home, the fam asked if I'd ordered from the local taqueria. Talk about a coup! Flautas are those addictive deep-fried skinny tacos. This version became a total repeat-recipe hit. I call them "fake-out" because unlike their messy, deep-fried cousins, they are a quick low-fat, baked, vegetarian gem of a recipe. Serve with Guacamole (opposite), the ultimate scoopable flavor bomb. **PHOTO ON PAGE 114**

12 corn tortillas

6 ounces Monterey Jack cheese, grated

2 tomatoes, chopped

One 15-ounce can black beans, drained and rinsed

½ teaspoon coarse salt

Juice of ½ lime

1 tablespoon safflower or other vegetable oil

1 Preheat the oven to 425°F with the racks in the upper and lower third positions. Lay out the tortillas on two rimmed baking sheets and scatter the cheese over them. Place in the oven for 1 to 2 minutes to melt the cheese.

2 Meanwhile, toss the tomatoes, black beans, salt, and lime juice together in a bowl.

3 Distribute the bean mixture evenly over the melted cheese and roll up the tortillas. Arrange side by side, seam side down, on one baking sheet. Brush the oil over the tops. Bake for 8 minutes, or until golden and crispy. ∗

Oven-Frying Versus Deep-Frying

Any deep-fried food, such as these flautas or Potato Poppers (page 214), that can be reasonably replicated by oven-frying is worth a try. Oven-frying is easier to do and doesn't require the careful handling that deep-frying does (see page 135). Here are a few tips:

- Coat the food with items that create a wowie crunch like panko bread crumbs (see page 17) or crushed tortilla chips.

- Brush a light coating of oil to coat the surface of the food before putting it in the oven.

- Preheat your metal baking pan in the oven before the food is added; this will help you achieve that audible sizzle-sear right off the bat.

- Broil for the last few minutes of cooking to finish with a golden touch.

queso fundido

serves 2

There are few things more divinely swoon-worthy than this concoction, which should almost be labeled an illegal substance. Queso fundido is insanely easy to replicate at home, and you'll be spared any cleanup hassle, because every last bit of the crispy cheese that crusts up at the bottom of the pan will be scraped up and devoured. Serve with tortillas and Roasted Salsa Verde (page 211).

4 ounces smoked chorizo, cut into ¼-inch pieces

½ small yellow onion, finely chopped

12 ounces Monterey Jack cheese, shredded

Eight 6-inch corn tortillas, warmed over a flame (see Note)

1. Preheat the broiler. Cook the chorizo in a 6-inch ovenproof skillet over medium heat until the fat begins to render, about 2 minutes. Add the onions and cook, stirring occasionally, until they soften and become translucent, about 3 minutes. Stir in the cheese.

2. Transfer the skillet to the broiler and broil until the cheese is bubbly and golden brown in places, 2 minutes. Serve immediately, with the tortillas. *

SMOKED CHORIZO

Spanish smoked chorizo is made from ground pork seasoned with smoked paprika (pimentón) and salt and then cured by hanging for 3 months. It should not be confused with its fresh, raw cousin, which needs to be cooked. The small firm links will keep for a long time in the refrigerator. A little goes a long way: dice one and add to scrambled eggs, frittatas (see page 38), or hash browns (see page 40) for a big flavor boost.

I like to toast the tortillas first to get that charred edge, then stack them to steam and become pliable for use. Toast them one at a time, on a direct flame or in a hot skillet or *comal* (a smooth flat Mexican griddle) until the edges start to darken, about 1 minute; flip and toast for another minute (some will puff up once you flip them). If they seem too toasted, almost crisp, stack them on top of one another wrapped in a cloth. To keep them fresh for 30 minutes, wrap the cloth stack in foil and keep in a warm place.

caramelized onion and bacon dip

makes 2 cups

If you love yet hate that packaged onion soup mix dip, this is the version for you. It is a richer, deeper-flavored, cleaner-ingredient excuse for a potato-chip-dipping marathon. Or smear it over Herb Flatbreads (page 122) for a classier affair. For a sip with your dip, try Grapefruit Thyme Cocktail (page 245). The dip can be refrigerated for up to 3 days.

¼ cup extra virgin olive oil

3 pounds yellow onions, halved lengthwise and thinly sliced crosswise

1 teaspoon coarse salt

2 tablespoons white wine vinegar

⅓ pound bacon, chopped

1½ cups mayonnaise

1 cup sour cream

OPTIONAL GARNISH

¼ cup safflower oil

3 shallots, thinly sliced into rings

1 Heat a large skillet. Add the olive oil (see Note, page 171). When it shimmers, add the onions and salt and cook over low heat, stirring occasionally, until the onions are deep golden in color, 45 minutes to 1 hour; add a little water if needed to prevent sticking. Add the vinegar during the last minute of cooking. Let cool.

2 Meanwhile, cook the bacon in a small skillet until it has rendered its fat. Using a slotted spoon, transfer the bacon to a paper-towel-lined plate; reserve the fat in the pan if you will be frying the shallots. Let the bacon cool.

3 Stir together the mayonnaise, sour cream, onions, and bacon in a large bowl.

4 For the optional garnish, add the vegetable oil to the skillet with the bacon fat and heat over medium-high heat until the oil shimmers. Add the shallots, lower the heat, and cook, stirring occasionally, until golden brown, about 2 minutes. Drain the shallots on a paper-towel-lined plate.

5 Garnish the dip with the fried shallots, if using, and serve. *

GOOD TO KNOW

Fried Alliums You don't really need fried shallots on top of this dip, or fried leeks on top of the Greek salad (see page 107). But you want them! Take a cue from the onion rings (see page 134), and a simple recipe ascends to a whole new level. Frying little onion bits until golden and crunchy will definitely take you there.

OPPOSITE: Herb Flatbreads (page 122) and Caramelized Onion and Bacon Dip (above)

herb flatbreads

makes twelve 6-inch flatbreads

Pizza-parlor dough is a quick road to a "home-baked" bread. For these flatbreads, just portion out the dough, roll into balls, stretch into rounds, season, and char on both sides: this can be done in a cast-iron skillet or other heavy pan or on the grill. Try serving the flatbreads with Caramelized Onion and Bacon Dip (page 120). **PHOTO ON PAGE 121**

1 pound pizza dough—thawed frozen store-bought or from the pizza parlor

Extra virgin olive oil for rolling the dough

2 garlic cloves, minced

2 tablespoons finely chopped fresh parsley

1 tablespoon finely chopped fresh oregano

2 teaspoons flaky sea salt, such as Maldon, or coarse salt

⅛ teaspoon red pepper flakes

1 Oil a rimmed baking sheet. On a lightly floured work surface, divide the dough into 12 pieces. With lightly oiled hands, roll each piece into a ball and transfer to the baking sheet.

2 Combine the garlic, parsley, oregano, salt, and red pepper flakes in a small bowl.

3 Heat a large cast-iron or other heavy skillet over medium-high heat. Hold a piece of dough in midair and stretch it into a 6-inch circle with your fingers, then place in the skillet, sprinkle with a pinch of the herb mixture, and cook undisturbed until the dough bubbles and blackens in spots on the bottom, about 1½ minutes. Flip and continue cooking until blackened in spots on the second side, about 1 minute more. (If using a grill, cooking time totals 5 minutes.) Transfer to a serving board or platter and repeat with the remaining dough. Serve warm or at room temperature. ∗

Flatbread

Many cultures have their own versions of flatbread, the perfect platform for all manner of savory and sweet toppings and fillings.

Injera . . . . Ethiopia
Tortilla . . . . Mexico
Chapati . . . . India
Lavash . . . . Armenia
Matzoh . . . . Middle East
Pita . . . . Greece
Blintz . . . . Russia
Crepe . . . . France
Pizza . . . . Italy

loaded potato skins

makes 12 potato skins

When my oldest son, Calder, went off to college, I was a little nervous about how he would fare foodwise. My suspicions were realized by the first culinary report I got describing the previous night's "amazing" dinner—take-out chicken wings and delivery pizza. I thought living off this type of food sounded disgusting but tried my best to understand his newfound habits—and I realized that even though college students can hardly be considered to have discriminating palates, they're onto something. Familiar foods that make us happy transport us back to our earliest tastes of deliciousness, memories often associated with pleasure and peace. So I started making this sort of recipe whenever he came home, based on ingredients like chicken and potatoes. Needless to say, this potato-based dish is hedonistically delicious, and only an active someone the age of a college student could handle a steady diet of these calories. **PHOTO ON PAGE 124**

6 large russet (baking) potatoes (about 3½ pounds), scrubbed

6 slices bacon

⅓ cup extra virgin olive oil

1 teaspoon coarse salt

¼ teaspoon white pepper

4 ounces sharp white cheddar cheese, shredded

4 ounces Monterey Jack cheese, shredded

1 cup sour cream

¼ cup chopped fresh chives

1 Preheat the oven to 375°F with a rack in the center position. Prick each potato several times with a fork (see Note) and bake for about 1 hour, until the potatoes can be easily pierced with a toothpick. Remove from the oven and raise the oven temperature to 450°F.

2 Meanwhile, cook the bacon in a large skillet until crisp. Transfer to a paper-towel-lined plate to drain. Chop the bacon and set aside.

3 When the potatoes are cool enough to handle, halve them lengthwise and scoop out most of the flesh, leaving a ¼-inch-thick layer of flesh attached to the skins. Reserve the scooped flesh for another use, such as mashed potatoes.

4 Brush the skins with the olive oil and season with the salt and pepper. Place skin side down on a rimmed baking sheet and bake for 18 to 20 minutes, until crisp and golden.

5 Scatter the cheeses and bacon over the skins and bake 5 minutes more, until the cheese is melted and bubbly. Dollop with the sour cream and chives and serve. ✳

NOTE Prick the potatoes in order to avoid a possible explosion. As I've learned the hard way, raw potatoes really have to be pricked before baking.

teriyaki-glazed wings

serves 4 normal people or 2 college students

I'm a wing girl—always have been—and for the longest time that was never a family conflict. With any given roasted whole chicken dinner, there was no dispute: Mom got the wings. But over the years, my family caught on to the skin-crunch-meat-bone wing attributes, and now they all want the wings. So we buy large pallets of them in the grocery store for home cooking. For a straight-up collegiate-style chow-down, serve with Loaded Potato Skins (page 123).

GLAZE

⅔ cup low-sodium soy sauce

1⅓ cups sake or dry white wine

¼ cup mirin

One 1-inch piece ginger, peeled and minced

2 garlic cloves, minced

2 tablespoons sugar

2 pounds whole chicken wings

1 tablespoon vegetable oil

½ teaspoon coarse salt

1 Preheat the oven to 375°F with a rack in the center position. For the glaze, combine the soy sauce, sake, mirin, ginger, garlic, and sugar in a small saucepan and boil until reduced to ½ cup, about 15 minutes. Transfer to a bowl and let cool to room temperature.

2 Toss the wings with the oil and salt in a bowl and transfer to a rimmed baking sheet. Bake for 30 minutes, then brush generously with the glaze. Bake for 15 minutes, basting and turning every 5 minutes until the wings look caramelized. *

WING VARIATIONS

Hot wings, garlic wings, honey-mustard wings, barbecue wings, and teriyaki wings are being scarfed down all over the country. Analyze your favorite take-out tastes and replicate the flavors at home, using the basic cook time given here. For instance, honey-mustard-glazed wings are easy: whisk equal parts of honey and your favorite mustard, add some lemon juice, and you're set. When using most glazes, you want to get the wings cooked and golden before adding the glaze, or it will burn before the chicken is cooked through—and the result won't be as crunchy.

OPPOSITE: Loaded Potato Skins (page 123) and Teriyaki-Glazed Wings (above)

street-corner pretzels

makes 12 pretzels

On my very first trip to New York City, the first thing I noticed when I emerged from the train station was the aroma of roasting chestnuts wafting from a vendor's cart. Also on offer were big, fluffy, salty, doughy pretzels. You can still find the same type of pretzel everywhere on the streets of New York. One pound store-bought bread dough can be used in place of the homemade.

1 cup warm water

2 teaspoons sugar

¼ teaspoon coarse salt

One ¼-ounce package (2¼ teaspoons) active dry yeast

3 cups all-purpose flour, plus more for dusting

2 tablespoons unsalted butter, at room temperature

3 tablespoons baking soda

2 tablespoons pretzel salt or coarse salt

Mustard

1 Combine the water, sugar, salt, and yeast in a small bowl and let stand for about 5 minutes to dissolve the yeast.

2 Put the flour in a large bowl. Using a pastry cutter or your fingers, cut the butter into the flour until the mixture resembles coarse crumbs. Slowly pour in the yeast mixture, stirring to combine. Using your hands, gather the dough together, turn it out onto a lightly floured surface, and knead until it is no longer sticky, about 5 minutes. Cover with plastic and let rise for 30 minutes.

3 Cut the dough into 12 pieces. One at a time, roll each one into an 18-inch-long rope. Form a U shape, and twist the ends together twice. Fold the twisted portion backward over the center of the U shape to form a circle, then gently press the ends of the rope onto the dough to seal. Transfer to an oiled baking sheet (you will probably need two). Let rise for 20 minutes.

4 Preheat the oven to 475°F with a rack in the center position. Bring a large pot of water to a boil and add the baking soda.

5 Boil the pretzels in batches, without crowding them, until puffed and slightly shiny, 1 to 2 minutes per side. Transfer to wire racks to drain.

6 Return the pretzels to the baking sheet and sprinkle with the pretzel salt. Bake for about 15 minutes, until golden brown and puffed up; the pretzels will keep, uncovered, at room temperature for up to 12 hours. Rewarm in a 250°F oven if desired, and serve with your favorite mustard. *

GOOD TO KNOW

Pretzel making, like bagel making, involves both boiling and baking. The boiling cooks the interior of the dough for the initial puff and creates a chewy texture. Adding baking soda to the boiling water alkalizes it, which accounts for the shiny brown crust and unique flavor. You must drain the boiled pretzels on wire racks, but don't let too much time elapse before baking, or the pretzels will deflate. The ideal baked pretzel is soft inside with a thin, golden outside layer that is firm and slightly crunchy.

sicilian-style deep-dish pizza

serves 4 to 6

This beautiful soft yeast dough is the basis for a Chicago-style deep-dish pizza or what they call a Sicilian in New York City pizza parlors. Basically it's a thick, doughy, focaccia-like crust instead of the thin, crispy, and chewy variety. This one, baked with one of my favorite toppings of all time—slow-roasted tomatoes—rather than laden with mozzarella, harks back to my grandmother's house, where she and her sisters embedded this scent and taste memory in my mind. The tomatoes can be made in advance, as can the dough, which needs to rise overnight in the refrigerator. Then simply roll out the dough, let it rest, and assemble the pizza just before baking.

PIZZA DOUGH

1⅓ cups water

1 teaspoon sugar

One ¼-ounce package (2¼ teaspoons) active dry yeast

3 cups plus 1 tablespoon all-purpose flour

¼ cup cornmeal

1 teaspoon coarse salt

¼ cup olive oil, plus more for the bowl

Slow-Roasted Tomatoes (recipe follows)

¼ cup grated Parmesan or Pecorino Romano cheese

1 Combine the water, sugar, and yeast in a medium bowl and let stand for 3 to 4 minutes to dissolve the yeast.

2 Whisk together 3 cups of the flour, the cornmeal, and salt in another medium bowl. Slowly add one-third of the flour mixture to the yeast mixture, stirring with a wooden spoon; then add another third and stir. Add the olive oil, then the remaining flour, and stir.

3 Sprinkle the remaining tablespoon of flour on a countertop, turn out the dough, and knead until smooth. Transfer the dough to a large oiled bowl and turn to coat in oil. Cover and let rise overnight in the refrigerator.

4 The next day, oil a rimmed baking sheet. On a lightly floured board, roll the dough out to the size of the pan. Fit the dough into the pan and let rest for 30 minutes.

5 Preheat the oven to 450°F with a rack in the center position. Spread the tomatoes evenly over the dough. Bake for about 30 minutes, until the tomatoes are bubbling and the dough is golden brown. Remove from the oven and sprinkle on the grated cheese. ∗

slow-roasted tomatoes

makes 4 to 6 cups

These can be made up to 2 days ahead.

12 medium tomatoes,
sliced ¼ inch thick

4 shallots, thinly sliced

10-12 thyme sprigs

½ cup olive oil

1 teaspoon coarse salt

1 Preheat the oven to 300°F with a rack in the center position. Arrange the tomatoes in a single layer on two baking sheets. Scatter the shallots and thyme sprigs over the tomatoes, drizzle with the olive oil, and sprinkle with the salt.

2 Roast for 2 to 2½ hours, turning the tomatoes a few times, until wilted and browning in places. Let cool. Store in a sealed container in the refrigerator. *

GOOD
TO
KNOW

Slow-roasted tomatoes are very versatile.

- Toss into cooked pasta for dinner.

- Spread over garlic crostinis (see page 109) for an appetizer.

- Chop and stir into chicken broth for roasted tomato soup.

- Swap for (or add to) the peppers in Sausage and Pepper Salad with Golden Crostini (page 109).

- Serve as a side dish with roasted or grilled meats.

- Tuck into an omelet with some grated mozzarella cheese.

- Layer into a sandwich with sharp cheddar cheese and sliced roast beef.

sun-dried tomato–parmesan crisps

makes 24 crisps

These savory nibbles—inspired by 'wichcraft, a take-out lunch spot near my office—are great appetizers with wine. Or serve them with Classic Tomato Soup (page 61). Using that versatile convenience item, frozen puff pastry, makes them easy to put together. If you can't find sun-dried tomato paste (see page 23), substitute good-quality regular tomato paste.

3 tablespoons sun-dried tomato paste

1 tablespoon extra virgin olive oil

1 piece store-bought puff pastry (such as a 17.3-ounce package Pepperidge Farm), thawed

½ cup grated Parmesan cheese

¼ teaspoon freshly ground black pepper

1 Preheat the oven to 375°F with a rack in the center position. Combine the tomato paste and olive oil in a small bowl.

2 On a lightly floured surface, roll out the puff pastry to a 12-inch square. Transfer to a parchment-lined baking sheet.

3 Spread the tomato paste mixture evenly over the pastry with a rubber spatula. Sprinkle with the cheese and pepper. Using a pizza wheel or a sharp knife, cut into quarters in one direction and then into sixths in the other, to make 24 pieces.

4 Bake for 20 to 22 minutes, until puffed and golden. Transfer to a wire rack and cool to room temperature before serving. ∗

FREEZER FRIEND

Puff pastry is one of the heavy lifters of convenience items. Whether your garden-variety puff pastry sheets, resplendent with the impolitic ingredients of vegetable shortening and high-fructose corn syrup, or artisanal brands like Dufour (www.dufourpastrykitchens.com) that are made with all butter, frozen puff pastry is a boon to home cooks. Different fillings and shapes become old-fashioned cocktail canapés like pigs in a blanket or mini-spinach triangles. Dessert turnovers need only a scoop of jam or a chocolate square wrapped inside a rolled-out 4-inch square of pastry and baked for 20 minutes at 400°F.

cheddar drop biscuits

makes 18 biscuits

Your only problem with these great biscuits will be the irresistible force drawing you to eat too many, especially when they're still warm. You can use this good, reliable recipe any time you're craving a moist and savory drop biscuit. I love to serve these with Butterfield Stageline Chili (page 156), broken up into little pieces and stirred into the bowl. You can also keep them at the ready wrapped in resealable plastic bags in the freezer—reheat in a 275°F oven for 5 minutes, or let defrost at room temperature for 30 minutes before heating in the microwave briefly. Reheated frozen biscuits taste just like fresh-baked. **PHOTO ON PAGE 157**

2 cups all-purpose flour

2 teaspoons baking powder

½ teaspoon baking soda

1 teaspoon sugar

½ teaspoon coarse salt

Pinch of cayenne pepper

6 tablespoons cold unsalted butter, cut into small cubes

6 ounces sharp white or orange cheddar cheese, shredded

1⅓ cups buttermilk (shaken well before measuring)

2 tablespoons chopped fresh chives

1 Preheat the oven to 425°F with the racks in the upper and lower third positions. Line two baking sheets with parchment.

2 Whisk together the flour, baking powder, baking soda, sugar, salt, and cayenne in a large bowl. Work in the butter with a pastry cutter or your fingers until the butter is incorporated but some pea-sized lumps remain. Stir in the cheddar, then add the buttermilk and chives, stirring just until the dough comes together.

3 Using two large spoons, drop ¼ cupfuls of the dough onto the prepared baking sheets, spaced 2 inches apart. Bake for 12 to 14 minutes, rotating the baking sheets once, until golden brown. Serve warm. ∗

GOOD TO KNOW

If you're serving these with chili, you can drop the batter in large dollops right on top of the chili pot about 15 minutes before the chili is done. The result will be a moist, soft version instead of the crunchy contrast of oven-baked biscuits. Scoop up a cheddar "dumpling" with each portion of chili. I even drop smaller dollops of this dough over my favorite chicken chowder as it cooks, for quick chicken and dumplings.

english muffin tidbits

serves 6 to 8

Straight from my grandmother's recipe file, title and all, these little bites have all the flavor and appeal of an everything bagel, what with the poppy seeds, garlic, and onion. Serve with soups or alongside some cheese for nibbling.

6 English muffins

8 tablespoons (1 stick) unsalted butter, at room temperature

1 garlic clove, minced

1 small onion, minced

1 teaspoon poppy seeds

1 Preheat the broiler. Split the English muffins open and spread with the butter. Combine the garlic and onion and sprinkle evenly over the muffins. Sprinkle on the poppy seeds.

2 Arrange the muffins on a baking sheet and broil until lightly golden. Serve warm. *

ENGLISH MUFFINS

English muffins are one of the great shortcut foods. Whoever coined the term "nooks and crannies" to describe their mini-potholes, which capture melting butter, peanut butter, honey, or jam, deserves an award. English muffins are also an excellent burger bun alternative. The hamburger patty sandwiched inside oozes its juicy, beefy condiment runoff into those same nooks and crannies.

---

crispy crunchy onion rings

serves 4

Faced with a choice between French fries and onion rings, my crunchy side will always choose onion rings. Something about onion rings just puts me over the edge—perhaps it's the crunch of the fried coating surrounding the soft-sweet slivers of onion. Soaking the onions in cold water for 10 minutes will dilute their sulphur content, making them sweeter and milder.

2 large Vidalia or other mild onions, cut into ¼-inch-wide rings

Vegetable oil for deep-frying

1 cup plus 2 tablespoons all-purpose flour

¼ cup cornstarch

2 teaspoons baking powder

1 teaspoon coarse salt, plus more to taste

1⅓ cups ice-cold water

1 Put the onions in a large bowl filled with cold water and soak for 10 minutes.

2 Heat 2 inches of oil to 365°F in a deep heavy-bottomed pot or prepare your electric deep-fryer.

3 Whisk together the flour, cornstarch, baking powder, and salt in a medium bowl. Whisk in the ice-cold water and set the bowl of batter in a bowl of ice.

4 Drain the onions well and dry thoroughly between layers of paper towels. Working with one handful at a time, dip the onions in the batter, allowing the excess to drip back into the bowl, and carefully place in the oil. Fry, turning once, until crisp and golden, about 3 minutes per batch. Transfer to a paper-towel-lined tray to drain, and sprinkle with salt. *

HOW TO PULL IT OFF

All fried onion rings are not created equal. The batter must be light, not thick and gloppy—this is achieved by the correct proportion of flour to water. The final product must be crispy, not cakey; here the cornstarch promotes crunchiness. Use sweet Vidalia onions or another similar mild-mannered onion. And the onions should not be cut too thick. Make sure you have a sharp knife and a firm grip (fingertips turned under, please). Cook fast and hot—oil management is crucial to success. A deep-fry/candy thermometer is a good investment if you deep-fry often—you can also use it for Brined and Fried Chicken (page 170) and Candied Apples (page 281).

deep-frying

I understand it can be daunting to face a vat of hot oil with visions of singed hair and fire swirling in your head, but it's time to get over your fear of deep-frying! If you already love to cook fried foods, buy a commercial deep-fryer; they are available for under $100 and are foolproof. But if you fry rarely, you just need to follow a few simple rules for success and safety.

- Choose the right oil, like safflower, canola, or peanut, which will not smoke at the desired frying temperature of 350°F to 380°F.

- Use a thermometer. Ideally you want to fry at 350°F. Bear in mind that when the cold food enters the hot oil, the temperature will drop so get the oil to 380°F before adding the food to compensate for the drop. And do not overcrowd the pan, or the temperature will drop dramatically and the food will suck up the oil rather than be fried in it. Keep the oil temperature no lower than 350°F (but up to 370°F) during cooking by regulating the heat underneath on the stove.

- Choose the right pan—a heavy deep pot—and don't overfill the pan. Leave at least 2 inches of space between the top of the oil and the top of the pan.

- Keep any water—for instance, on a recently cleaned but undried utensil—away from the oil to avoid splattering. As everyone knows, oil and water do not mix, especially hot oil and cold water!

- Do not reuse the oil. Discard it responsibly by placing it in a sealable container after it cools and putting it in the nonrecycling trash bin.

- Last but not least, have a fire extinguisher nearby in the event of an accident—and make sure you know how to use it.

When foods are fried correctly, the outside will be sealed into a crispy (not oily) crust while inside the food steams itself.

shrimp summer rolls

makes 12 rolls

Summer rolls are a healthful way to satisfy an Asian food craving. They are fresh room-temperature rolls, not deep-fried. Here, julienned veggies (see page 83), blanched shrimp, herbs, and thin noodles are wrapped in rice papers and served with a flavorful dipping sauce. Set up an assembly line to make them—it's a great family activity.

24 medium shrimp (about 1 pound)

Coarse salt

4 ounces rice vermicelli noodles

12 spring roll skins

1 cup fresh Thai basil leaves or Italian basil leaves

1 packed cup finely shredded Napa cabbage

1 medium carrot, peeled and julienned

DIPPING SAUCE

3 garlic cloves, minced

1 jalapeño, minced

¼ cup chopped palm sugar or packed light brown sugar

Juice of 2 limes (¼ cup)

⅓ cup fish sauce

2 scallions, white and pale green parts minced, dark green tops thinly sliced

1 Put a large pot of water over high heat. Meanwhile, peel and devein the shrimp. When the water comes to a boil, add a generous pinch of salt, then add the shrimp, and cook until opaque, about 2 minutes. Using a slotted spoon or spider, transfer the shrimp to a bowl of ice water. This will stop the cooking and ensure the shrimp remain tender and moist.

2 Put the noodles in a baking dish, cover with hot water, and soak until softened, 8 to 10 minutes. Drain in a colander and rinse under cold water.

3 Cut the shrimp in half lengthwise. Pour ½ inch of cool water into a pie plate. Submerge a spring roll skin in the water for 10 seconds, then remove and transfer to a clean work surface. Place 4 shrimp halves cut side up in a straight row across the lower third of the skin. Top the shrimp with a few basil leaves, a few tablespoons of the shredded cabbage, a pinch of the carrots, and ⅓ cup of the rice noodles. Carefully lift the edge of the spring roll skin nearest you up and over the filling. Fold the sides over, and continue to roll up. Transfer to a platter, seam side down, and cover with a damp paper towel. Continue building the remaining rolls.

4 For the dipping sauce, whisk the garlic, jalapeño, sugar, lime juice, fish sauce, and minced scallions in a medium bowl. Transfer to individual dipping bowls and garnish with the sliced scallion tops.

5 Serve the summer rolls with the dipping sauce. *

Summer Roll Salad When a friend with three young boys—so no time for wrapping and rolling—saw me making these, she commented that she'd rather just dump all the elements in a bowl, mix it with the dipping sauce, and call it a salad. We tried it, and it's a great idea.

ramen noodle upgrade

serves 1

My son Calder's all-time favorite late-night snack is only in need of a small pot of boiling water. He figures that even a single guy who gets home late, when the local pizza joint and corner deli are closed, needs to eat. Starving and desperate—with no options left? This recipe is a clever abbreviated adaptation of the favorite Chinese takeout cold sesame noodles.

One 3-ounce package ramen noodles with flavoring

1 tablespoon soy sauce

2 tablespoons chunky peanut butter

2 teaspoons Sriracha sauce

½ scallion, thinly sliced (optional)

Boil the noodles with the flavor pack as directed; drain off most of the liquid. Toss with the soy sauce, peanut butter, and Sriracha. Garnish with the scallion, if you like, and eat immediately. *

CRUNCHY PEANUT BUTTER SNACKING

Keep a good variety of this on hand, and it will afford you many different munchable moments.

- Make a PB&J, adding apple slices.
- Dollop over vanilla ice cream.
- Spread on a rice cake.
- Blend in a smoothie.
- Use as a dip for a frozen banana.
- Stuff in a celery stick.

GOOD TO KNOW

Asian Ingredients A little planning-ahead allows you to transform the way you cook at home. Once your pantry is stocked with a few specialty items like the rice noodles and wrappers, all that stands between you and seemingly exotic homemade takeout are a few everyday supermarket ingredients. See Asian Pantry, page 16.

beef satay with thai peanut sauce

makes 20 skewers; serves 6 to 8

Take your young kids to a Thai restaurant, and one of them is sure to order satay. The marinated meat, whether chicken or beef, is threaded on skewers and grilled, but it's the creamy peanut sauce that really grabs their attention. These skewers will be a smash hit at your table. Thinly sliced boneless chicken can be substituted for the beef.

¼ cup peanut oil

1 large shallot, minced

2 garlic cloves, minced

One 2-inch piece ginger, peeled and minced

¼ cup low-sodium soy sauce

1 teaspoon turmeric

1 teaspoon ground coriander

¼ cup fresh lime juice

¼ teaspoon freshly ground black pepper

1 pound flank steak, sliced ⅛ inch thick against the grain (see page 68)

Thai Peanut Sauce (recipe follows)

About 20 wooden skewers

1 Whisk together the peanut oil, shallot, garlic, ginger, soy sauce, turmeric, coriander, lime juice, and pepper in an 8-inch square baking dish or wide shallow bowl. Add the beef, tossing to combine, and marinate up to 1 hour at room temperature, or up to 4 hours in the fridge.

2 Meanwhile, soak the skewers in water for 30 minutes (see Note); drain.

3 Preheat an outdoor grill or a grill pan over medium-high heat. Thread 1 slice of beef onto each skewer. Grill the beef, turning once, just until cooked through, about 2 minutes total. Serve with the peanut sauce. ∗

NOTE

Wooden skewers must always be soaked in water before using on a grill. Otherwise, the wood will burn before the meat is cooked.

thai peanut sauce

makes about 3 cups

1 cup plus 1 tablespoon unsalted
roasted peanuts

1 garlic clove, smashed and peeled

2 tablespoons finely chopped
palm sugar or light brown sugar

2 tablespoons fish sauce

1 tablespoon low-sodium soy sauce

1½ cups unsweetened coconut milk

1 teaspoon Asian sesame oil

1 tablespoon fresh lime juice

¼ cup unsweetened shredded coconut

1 Combine 1 cup of the peanuts
with the remaining ingredients in
a blender and blend until smooth.
Transfer to a serving bowl.

2 Chop the remaining tablespoon
of peanuts and sprinkle over the
sauce before serving. ∗

what's for dinner?

main dishes • 145
noodles, rice, and corn • 185
veggies and other sides • 213

MAIN DISHES

PRECEDING SPREAD: Roasting the vegetables for Salsa Roja (page 208);
OPPOSITE: Eggplant Parm Stacks (page 146).

eggplant parm stacks

serves 8

This fabulous take on the traditional "eggplant Parm"—a staple of red-sauce Italian joints—will be a revelation. Forget about the heavy, greasy eggplant lost in deep-fried breading. Here it is grilled to a soft-charred beauty and layered with melted cheese, seasoned bread crumbs, and a delicate tomato sauce. This recipe began as an attempt to convert my husband, who was scarred as a youth when forced to eat eggplant at its slimy-viscous-undercooked worst. As a result, he refers to eggplant as the organ meat of vegetables. Not fair. Whenever he's out, I cook eggplant!

2 eggplants (2½ pounds total), sliced ⅓ inch thick (24 slices total)

⅓ cup plus 1 tablespoon extra virgin olive oil

1 teaspoon coarse salt

1 cup fine bread crumbs

½ cup grated Parmesan cheese

¼ teaspoon freshly ground black pepper

1 tablespoon finely chopped fresh oregano

¼ cup chopped fresh basil

3 cups Italian Tomato Sauce (recipe follows) or other tomato sauce

A 1-pound ball fresh mozzarella, halved lengthwise and sliced crosswise ¼ inch thick (24 slices total)

1 Preheat the oven to 375°F with a rack in the center position. Preheat a grill or grill pan over medium-high heat.

2 Brush the eggplant slices on both sides with ⅓ cup of the olive oil and season with the salt. Working in batches, add to the grill pan and cook, flipping once, until charred and soft, 10 to 12 minutes. Transfer to a platter or baking sheet.

3 Combine the bread crumbs, Parmesan, pepper, herbs, and the remaining tablespoon of olive oil in a medium bowl.

4 Place 8 slices of the grilled eggplant on a parchment-lined rimmed baking sheet. Top each with 2 tablespoons tomato sauce, 1 tablespoon of the bread crumb mixture, and a slice of mozzarella. Repeat to make 2 more layers.

5 Bake for about 30 minutes, until soft, golden, and bubbly. Serve immediately. ✱

italian tomato sauce

makes 3 cups, enough for 1 pound of pasta

This is my basic red sauce for pasta.

1½ tablespoons extra virgin olive oil

2 garlic cloves, minced

⅛ teaspoon red pepper flakes

One 28-ounce can whole plum tomatoes, pulsed in a blender to a semichunky consistency

½ teaspoon coarse salt

1 basil sprig (optional)

1 tablespoon unsalted butter (optional)

1 Heat a medium saucepan over medium heat. Swirl in the olive oil to coat the pan. When the oil shimmers, add the garlic and pepper flakes and stir constantly for 30 seconds, just long enough to release the garlic's fragrance; don't cook it to golden.

2 Stir in the tomatoes and salt, raise the heat to high, and bring to a boil, then reduce the heat and simmer, uncovered, for 30 minutes, until the sauce is slightly reduced and a deep tomato color. Add the basil sprig in the last 5 minutes of cooking, if using. Remove the basil before serving and swirl in the butter, if desired. ∗

light and fluffy meatballs

makes 30 meatballs; serves 6 to 8

In our house, we have different meatballs, depending on the occasion. Family recipes come first, but my favorite premium pizza parlor serves an addictive meatball appetizer that is very different from the versions made by my Italian grandmothers. These spheres of super-puffed ground meat cooked in tomato sauce are absolutely cloud-like and almost melt in your mouth. Surmising that ricotta cheese is the secret weapon, I've replicated them here.

2 tablespoons extra virgin olive oil

1 small yellow onion, finely chopped

5 slices white bread, crusts removed and torn into pieces (about 3 cups)

1 cup whole milk

1 pound ground beef chuck

1 pound ground pork

1 pound ground veal

1 pound whole-milk ricotta cheese

½ cup grated Parmesan cheese, plus more for serving

⅓ cup chopped fresh flat-leaf parsley

1 tablespoon chopped fresh oregano

2 teaspoons coarse salt

½ teaspoon freshly ground black pepper

2 large eggs

2 quarts Italian Tomato Sauce (opposite) or other similar tomato sauce

1 Heat a 12-inch skillet over medium-high heat. Add the olive oil. When it shimmers, add the onions and cook until soft but not colored, about 5 minutes. Transfer to a large bowl.

2 Combine the bread and milk in a bowl and let soak for 5 minutes.

3 Squeeze the excess milk from the bread and finely chop it. Add the bread to the onions along with all the remaining ingredients except the tomato sauce. Gently fold with your hands to incorporate the ingredients, but do not overmix or the meatballs will be tough.

4 Bring the tomato sauce to a simmer in a large deep skillet. With wet hands, pinch off ¼ cup of the meat mixture and gently form into a ball. Drop the meatball into the sauce; repeat. Cover the pan and simmer, stirring carefully—to avoid breaking the meatballs apart—a few times, until they are cooked through, about 30 minutes after putting the last meatball in the skillet.

5 Serve the meatballs with the sauce and grated Parmesan cheese. ∗

FREEZER FRIEND

Both the meatballs and the sauce can be made in advance, cooled, and frozen separately for versatile serving options. Formed meatballs can be kept in the refrigerator for up to 2 days until ready to cook. Or freeze them in rows on a parchment-lined baking sheet until firm and then transfer to freezer bags. Drop frozen meatballs directly into the sauce and simmer for 1 hour.

pasta with sausage meat sauce

serves 4 to 6; makes 2 quarts sauce

For a twist on your typical meat sauce, start with seasoned good sausage squeezed from its casings—a shortcut to deep flavor. Rosemary adds a hint of fresh herby-pineyness to the rich sauce. I make enough so I have an extra quart to freeze for a thaw-and-heat meal (the sauce will be ready in the time it takes to cook the pasta).

SAUSAGE MEAT SAUCE

2 tablespoons olive oil

1 pound sweet Italian sausages, removed from casings

1 pound spicy Italian sausages, removed from casings

1 small yellow onion, finely chopped

1 medium carrot, peeled and finely chopped

2 garlic cloves, minced

1 tablespoon tomato paste

Two 28-ounce cans whole plum tomatoes

One 6-inch rosemary sprig

1 pound pasta, such as bucatini or spaghetti

1 Heat a 4- to 5-quart saucepan over medium-high heat. Add the oil. When it shimmers, add the sausage and brown, breaking it up into small pieces, just until cooked through, about 5 minutes.

2 Add the onions, carrots, garlic, and tomato paste and cook, stirring occasionally, until the vegetables begin to soften, about 3 minutes. Stir in the tomatoes and rosemary, breaking up the tomatoes with the side of a spoon or with scissors. Bring to a boil, then reduce the heat, partially cover, and simmer, stirring occasionally, until the sauce thickens and reduces slightly, about 30 minutes.

3 Meanwhile, bring a large pot of water to a boil. When the sauce has 10 minutes left, add the pasta to the boiling water and cook until al dente.

4 Drain the pasta, toss with 4 cups of the sauce, and serve. (The remaining quart of sauce should be cooled, then transferred to a freezer-safe container with a tight-fitting lid; it can be frozen for up to 6 months.) ✳

FREEZER FRIEND

Make, don't buy, your very own convenience items. My freezer is like a train station: there is a constant rotation in and out. I'm always pulling out frozen things (chicken breasts, burger patties, wonton wrappers, etc.) to cook that night or freezing leftovers or putting just-made desserts in the freezer for later.

old-school meat loaf

serves 6

This recipe was one of the five meals my mom had in her heavy weeknight rotation to feed our family of six. I loved the way she made three holes in the loaf and filled each one with a reservoir of spicy ketchup, so each bite had a touch of it. Little details like a pool of ketchup create a memorable dinner experience for a little kid—never to be forgotten.

I grate the onions to avoid unpleasantly large chunks in the meat loaf; use a box grater and they'll melt into the meat mixture as it cooks. Grated carrots help keep the loaf moist.

½ cup fresh bread crumbs

⅓ cup whole milk

2 pounds ground beef chuck

¼ cup grated onion

1 carrot, peeled and grated

1 large egg

2 teaspoons coarse salt

½ teaspoon freshly ground black pepper

⅓ to ½ cup Chili Sauce (recipe follows) or regular bottled chili sauce

1 Preheat the oven to 325°F with a rack in the middle position. In a large bowl, soak the bread crumbs in the milk for 5 minutes.

2 Add the beef, onions, carrots, egg, salt, and pepper to the bread crumb mixture. Mix gently.

3 Shape the meat mixture into a loaf and put it in an 8 ½-by-4½-inch loaf pan. Make 3 holes, evenly spaced lengthwise, in the meat loaf and fill them to the top with the sauce. Bake for 40 to 45 minutes, until firm to the touch. Remove from the oven and let rest for 10 to 15 minutes.

4 Pour any accumulated juices over the top of the meat loaf. Slice and serve with the remaining chili sauce on the side. ✶

chili sauce

makes ¾ cup

½ cup ketchup

1 teaspoon chili paste, such as sambal oelek

¼ cup sweet pickle relish

Mix the ingredients together in a small bowl. ✶

LEFTOVERS

Meat loaf is my all-time favorite sandwich, but since there are never any leftovers to be had after this dinner, I always make 2 loaves. I'm very picky about my sandwich. Thick slices of white bread slathered with mayonnaise (I dropped the mustard smear over the years—it masked the flavor), topped with shredded (not torn) romaine lettuce and a big slab of the cold meat loaf dusted with coarse salt and freshly ground pepper. Every bite should be accompanied by the crunchy-sweet nibble of a bread-and-butter pickle chip.

tamale pie

serves 6

This recipe does away with the labor intensity of individual tamale prep. All the components of a good tamale are here, layered together in a large group-friendly casserole. Think of it like a Mexican-style shepherd's pie. If you're game for full-scale tamale making, see the recipe for Chicken or Cheese Tamales (page 207 or 210).

2 tablespoons extra virgin olive oil

1 medium yellow onion, chopped

1 green bell pepper, cored, seeded, and chopped

2 teaspoons coarse salt

1 tablespoon chopped fresh oregano or 2 teaspoons dried

1 teaspoon ground cumin

¼ teaspoon freshly ground black pepper

1 pound ground beef chuck

1 tablespoon tomato paste

One 15½-ounce can whole plum tomatoes

2½ cups water

1 cup fine cornmeal

3 ounces Monterey Jack cheese, grated

1 jalapeño, minced

2 ears yellow corn, kernels and milk stripped from cobs (see page 111), or 1½ cups frozen corn kernels

1 Preheat the oven to 375°F with a rack in the middle position. Heat a 10-inch cast-iron skillet over medium-high heat. Add the oil to the pan. When the oil shimmers, add the onions, bell pepper, and 1 teaspoon of the salt and cook until the vegetables are soft and golden in places, about 5 minutes.

2 Add the oregano, cumin, pepper, and ground beef and cook, stirring, just until the beef is cooked through, 4 to 5 minutes. Stir in the tomato paste and cook for 1 minute. Add the tomatoes, breaking them up with the side of the spoon, and simmer until the mixture is slightly thickened, about 5 minutes. Remove from the heat.

3 Bring the water to a boil in a medium saucepan. Stir in the cornmeal and the remaining 1 teaspoon salt and cook, stirring until thick and creamy, 2 minutes. Remove from the heat and stir in the cheese, jalapeño, and corn. Spread evenly over the beef mixture.

4 Transfer the pan to the oven and bake for 40 to 45 minutes, until the top is golden and the filling is bubbling around the edges of the pan. Let stand for 20 minutes before serving. *

ONE-PAN WONDER

For potlucks, anchoring a dinner party, or just feeding the family, one-dish meals like this—made in an oven-to-table vessel—are a godsend. Tamale Pie, Spinach Zucchini Lasagna (page 192), and Ham and Cheese Strata (page 36) need only a green salad to complete them for a delicious meal.

CHILIES

Let's get a few things straight about chilies (the peppers).

Commercial chili powder is generally a combination of ground dried red chili with ground cumin, dried oregano, dehydrated garlic and onions, and/or cayenne. Pure chili powders—made with a single type of ground dried red chili pepper, of which there are dozens of varieties—bring their own distinct flavor to the party. Fresh green or red chilies are another story: herbaceous, floral, and tangy, with varying degrees of heat. A great pot of chili results from the subtle combination of one or all of these.

Sometimes, however, I forgo commercial chili powder and instead deconstruct it, adding straight pure chili powder (sweet or hot), oregano, cumin, etc., along with a fresh green chili pepper (sweet or hot), chosen to complement the attributes of the dried red pepper (smoky, earthy, hot). This recipe uses the commercial powder but augments it with more herbs and spices. The fresh floral heat delivered by the Scotch bonnet or habañero chili heightens the whole.

butterfield stageline chili

serves 6 to 8

My chili recipes are like my kids—impossible to pick a favorite. A Bowl of Red (*Mad Hungry*, page 148), Chicken Chipotle (www.madhungry.com) and this-here youngest one, the Butterfield Stageline, all possess different personalities and attributes. And, like the boys, they alternate their moments in the sun. A persnickety cook friend recently switched from his own beloved recipe to this one. It stands out because of the ground pork and cubed beef brisket combination, which brings a texture, chew, and mouthfeel that I love in chili. This version comes from an old-time formula reputed to have fed stagecoach customers at way stations along the Butterfield line, which ran from St. Louis down through the Southwest and on to California. Cheddar Drop Biscuits (page 132), torn up and dragged through the sauciness, are all I need to complete it.

4 pounds beef brisket, cut into ½-inch pieces (see Note)

1 tablespoon plus 1 teaspoon coarse salt

½ teaspoon freshly ground black pepper

¼ cup extra virgin olive oil

2 pounds ground pork

2 large white onions, chopped

4 Anaheim chilies (6 ounces), chopped

1 Scotch bonnet or habañero chili, minced (seeds and ribs removed for less heat, if desired)

6 garlic cloves, minced

2 tablespoons tomato paste

2 tablespoons chopped fresh oregano

3 tablespoons chili powder

1 tablespoon ground cumin

Two 28-ounce cans whole plum tomatoes in juice

2 cups Chicken Broth (page 57) or store-bought beef broth

1 Season the brisket with the salt and pepper. Heat a Dutch oven over medium-high heat. Add 2 tablespoons of the oil and when it shimmers, add half the brisket. Brown, turning occasionally, for 4 to 5 minutes; transfer to a plate. Repeat with the remaining brisket.

2 Add the remaining 2 tablespoons oil to the pot, then add the pork, onions, chilies, and garlic and cook, stirring occasionally, until the pork is no longer pink and most of the liquid has evaporated, 6 to 8 minutes.

3 Stir in the tomato paste, oregano, chili powder, and cumin and cook for 2 minutes, until fragrant.

4 Puree 1 can of the tomatoes in a blender and stir into the chili, along with the remaining tomatoes and the chicken broth. Return the brisket to the pot. Bring to a boil, cover, reduce the heat, and simmer, stirring occasionally, until the beef is fork-tender, 3 to 3½ hours. Ladle into bowls and serve. ∗

NOTE This chunky chili uses brisket cut into medium pieces. If you don't have the time or patience to prep your meat that way, ask your butcher to do so. Most will be happy to accommodate you, especially if you give them a big smile.

OPPOSITE: Butterfield Stageline Chile (above) with Cheddar Drop Biscuits (page 132)

cowboy rib-eye steak

serves 4 to 6

Instead of individual rib-eye steaks, serving and slicing a large premium steak for a group is a more economical way to spread the wealth. You can replicate a Texas steak-house rib eye at home with this technique of pan-searing the meat and then finishing it in the oven. A garlicky spice rub counterbalances the sweetness of the brown sugar, which helps caramelize the meat. Differently delicious, skirt, hanger (pictured on the front jacket), and flank steak also love this rub—just cut the searing and roasting time in half.

1 tablespoon cumin seeds

1 tablespoon coriander seeds

2 teaspoons black peppercorns

2 tablespoons coarse salt

1 tablespoon sweet paprika

2 tablespoons light brown sugar

2 tablespoons finely chopped fresh oregano

5 garlic cloves, minced

One 3-pound bone-in rib-eye steak

1 Combine the cumin, coriander, and peppercorns in a spice grinder and pulse until coarsely ground. Transfer to a small bowl, add the salt, paprika, brown sugar, oregano, and garlic, and mix until combined.

2 Pat the steak thoroughly dry with paper towels and rub on all sides with the spice mixture. Let stand at room temperature for 1 hour, or as long as overnight in the refrigerator. If marinating in the refrigerator, remove the steak 1 hour before cooking to bring it to room temp.

3 Preheat the oven to 350°F with a rack in the middle position. Heat a large cast-iron pan over medium-high heat. Sear the steak on both sides until charred, 8 to 10 minutes total.

4 Transfer to the oven and roast for 18 to 20 minutes, or until an instant-read thermometer inserted into the center of the steak registers 125°F for medium-rare. Transfer to a carving board and let stand for at least 15 minutes before slicing and serving. *

Rib-eye Steak Rib eye is hands down my favorite cut of premium beef. You've got the bone imparting tons of flavor, and the perfect ratio of fat to meat, making it the ultimate "steak." I'm perfectly happy gnawing on the bone—with the little meaty bits attached to its crispy edges—leaving the meat for my fellow diners.

OPPOSITE: Cowboy Rib-Eye Steak (above) with Collard Greens with Ham and Bacon (page 225) and Candied Sweet Potatoes (page 221)

chicken-fried steak

serves 6

I don't have a Southern bone in my body, but I'm deeply attracted to the food of the South, which is all about cooking from the soul. Chicken-fried steak may not be chicken, but it is certainly steak, and it's most certainly fried, though shallow-fried. The steaks get smothered in a creamy white gravy made with the scrapings left in the pan. Smoky, buttery, sweet, and salty flavors are the name of the game. It's rich and fattening, literally not for the faint of heart. Serve with Candied Sweet Potatoes (page 221) and Collard Greens with Ham and Bacon (page 225).

2 pounds sirloin tip roast, cut into six ¾-inch-thick steaks

1½ teaspoons coarse salt

½ teaspoon freshly ground black pepper

1 cup plus 3 tablespoons all-purpose flour

¼ teaspoon cayenne pepper

1 cup buttermilk (well shaken before measuring)

Vegetable oil for panfrying

2 cups whole milk

1 Put the steaks on a clean work surface, cover with plastic wrap, and pound on both sides with the tenderizing side of a meat mallet until ¼ inch thick. Season the steaks with 1 teaspoon of the salt and ¼ teaspoon of the pepper.

2 Set a cooling rack over a baking sheet. Combine 1 cup of the flour and the cayenne in a wide shallow bowl and pour the buttermilk into another shallow bowl. Coat the steaks in flour, then in buttermilk, and again in flour; transfer to the baking sheet and let stand for 20 minutes

3 Heat a large cast-iron skillet over medium-high heat. Add ⅛ inch of oil. When it shimmers, fry the steaks in 2 batches, turning once, until golden brown on both sides, about 3 minutes per side. Transfer to a paper-towel-lined baking sheet or plate to drain.

4 Carefully pour all but 2 tablespoons of the fat from the skillet and return the pan to the heat. Whisk in the remaining 3 tablespoons flour and cook until bubbly and golden, 1 minute. Whisk in the whole milk and the remaining ½ teaspoon salt and ¼ teaspoon pepper, bring to a boil, whisking constantly, and boil until the gravy thickens slightly, about 1 minute. Transfer to a gravy boat or small pitcher.

5 Transfer the steaks to plates, pour the gravy over them, and serve immediately. ∗

HOW TO PULL IT OFF

Tenderizing Meat A sirloin tip roast and other less expensive yet flavorful cuts of meat require tenderizing, which can be achieved by marinating, pounding with a meat mallet, or both. When you pound the meat with a mallet, start in the middle and pound out to the edges to break down the tendons and thin the meat, which also shortens the cooking process.

pork tonkatsu

serves 4

Here crispy pork cutlets get dipped in a creamy yet light sauce made with thickened dashi (a Japanese vegetarian sea broth) and beaten eggs. Serve with cooked short-grain rice and Japanese Shredded Cabbage (page 237). **PHOTO ON PAGE 162**

Four 6-ounce pork loin cutlets

1 teaspoon coarse salt

¼ teaspoon freshly ground black pepper

½ cup all-purpose flour

2 large eggs, lightly beaten

1½ cups panko bread crumbs

DIPPING SAUCE

1 tablespoon safflower oil

1 small yellow onion, halved lengthwise and thinly sliced crosswise

2 cups Dashi (recipe follows)

⅓ cup mirin

⅓ cup soy sauce

5 scallions, sliced into 1-inch pieces

4 large eggs, lightly beaten

Vegetable oil for deep-frying

Garnishes: lemon wedges and toasted sesame seeds (see page 17)

1 Put the pork cutlets between sheets of plastic wrap and pound them to ½ inch thick with a meal mallet. Season both sides with the salt and pepper.

2 Set a cooling rack over a baking sheet. Put the flour, eggs, and panko in three separate wide shallow bowls. Dredge the pork slices in flour, then eggs, and then panko; transfer to the baking sheet. Let stand for at least 10 minutes, or up to 30 minutes.

3 Make the dipping sauce: Heat a large saucepan over medium-high heat. Add the safflower oil. When it shimmers, add the onions and sauté until translucent, about 3 minutes. Add the dashi, mirin, soy sauce, and scallions and bring to a boil. Remove from the heat and gradually stir in the eggs. Keep the sauce warm.

4 Heat 1½ inches of oil to 160°F in a deep heavy pot.

5 Fry the pork in 2 batches, turning a few times, until golden brown, 3 to 4 minutes per batch. Transfer to a paper-towel-lined plate to drain.

6 Slice the pork into 1-inch pieces. Serve with the sauce and garnishes. ∗

dashi

makes about 2½ quarts

Dashi is made with the seaweed called kombu (dried and packaged, it's a great item to keep in your pantry) and bonito fish flakes. Think of kombu as the meat-of-the-sea flavor base in the same way chicken or beef flavors a stock, and then think of the dried bonito flakes as the salty seasoning. This wonderful broth can be used for many soups. For one that's simple and nourishing, add cubed tofu, a few spinach leaves, slivered, and soba noodles.

2½ quarts water

Two 4-inch squares kombu

½ ounce bonito flakes

1 Combine the water and kombu in a saucepan and let stand for 30 minutes.

2 Bring the kombu and water to a bare simmer and cook gently for 10 minutes. Remove the kombu and add the bonito flakes. Boil for 5 minutes. Strain. ＊

{ NUTSHELL RECIPE: **miso soup**

Whisk 3 tablespoons miso (see page 16) into 1 quart hot dashi.
Stir in ⅓ pound cubed soft tofu and 2 thinly sliced scallions. ＊ }

OPPOSITE: Pork Tonkatsu (page 161) with Japanese Shredded Cabbage (page 237)
and Cold Soba Noodles with Dipping Sauce (page 198)

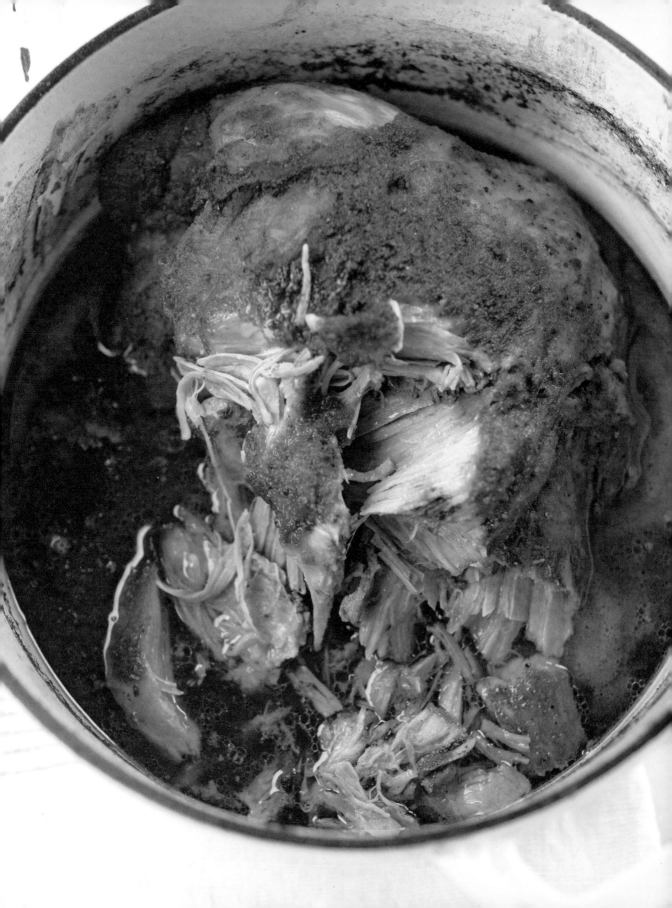

pulled pork

serves 6 to 8 as a main dish or makes enough for 8 to 10 sandwiches

Pork butt, or shoulder, is one of my favorite cuts of meat. It gives you excellent bang for your buck, since it flavorfully feeds a large crowd at a very affordable price. Just plan ahead for its 3- to 4-hour cooking time. Here it is rubbed with a spice mixture of cumin, paprika, salt, and pepper and braised in Guinness beer: no grill is needed to achieve that smoky barbecue-joint-worthy flavor. Serve on its own or with all the fixings: Collard Greens with Ham and Bacon (page 225), Creamy Chive Mashed Potatoes (page 215), and Cheddar Drop Biscuits (page 132). Or layer it into sandwiches with Classic Coleslaw (page 238). Either way, slather it with the tangy vinegar-based North Carolina–style barbecue sauce, which is thinner than most tomato-based barbecue sauces.

PULLED PORK

⅓ cup packed light brown sugar

1 tablespoon ground cumin

1 teaspoon paprika

1 tablespoon coarse salt

½ teaspoon freshly ground black pepper

One 6-pound boneless pork shoulder roast

24 ounces Guinness

6 garlic cloves, smashed and peeled

North Carolina BBQ Sauce (recipe follows)

1 For the pork, preheat the oven to 350°F with a rack in the lower third position. Combine the brown sugar, cumin, paprika, salt, and pepper in a small bowl.

2 Rub the spice mixture all over the pork. Put the pork fat side up in a 5- to 6-quart Dutch oven. Pour the Guinness over the meat. Add the garlic cloves and bring to a boil over high heat.

3 Cover the pot, transfer to the oven, and braise, basting a few times, for 3 to 4 hours, until the pork is fork-tender. Remove from the oven and shred the pork with two forks. Stir to incorporate with the braising liquid.

4 Serve with the barbecue sauce. *

north carolina bbq sauce

makes 1 cup

This sauce can be made up to 2 weeks ahead. Cool to room temperature, transfer to a container with a tight-fitting lid, and store in the refrigerator.

8 tablespoons (1 stick) unsalted butter

1 tablespoon tomato paste

2 tablespoons light brown sugar

1 teaspoon coarse salt

¼ teaspoon freshly ground black pepper

1 teaspoon cayenne pepper

½ cup apple cider vinegar

2 tablespoons fresh lemon juice

1 teaspoon hot sauce, such as Tabasco

Melt the butter in a medium saucepan over medium heat. Add the tomato paste, brown sugar, salt, pepper, cayenne, and vinegar, raise the heat, and boil, whisking constantly, until the sugar and salt dissolve, about 1 minute. Remove from the heat and whisk in the lemon juice and hot sauce. Let cool to room temperature before serving. ∗

the whole hog

For the past couple of years, our family has invested in a whole pig. It may sound crazy, but it makes a whole lot of sense. Ideally, you know where your animal was raised and by whom—what it ate and that its life and death unfolded in a humane fashion. As I've written before, ethics, ecology, and taste are one.

The meat comes to us butchered and wrapped in freezer paper, labeled with the cut and weight of each piece. In case you're wondering how much meat we're talking about: The first year, we bought a quarter pig, and all the meat fit neatly into two canvas L.L. Bean bags. Because that was gone within six weeks, we increased our take to a half hog the next year. The year after that, we took the whole animal: shoulders, loin and shoulder chops, hocks, ground pork, and more to defrost whenever we're ready. Over the years, I've discovered this naturally raised meat needs only salt and pepper for seasoning, and a sauté, fry, or braise for an utter porky deliciousness that no sauce could further enhance. We appreciate this sustainable meat and pay more (and eat less) for the privilege. And I don't have to buy meat of unknown origin at the supermarket.

For leads on where to buy a pig in your area,
consult www.localharvest.org.

lamb chops bathed in greek herbs

serves 4 to 6

Sometimes all you need to make something fabulous are fresh lemon, herbs, and garlic, a hallmark of Greek food—and its simplicity. I love the technique of grilling first to form a charred crust and then essentially marinating afterward, the hot meat absorbing the lemony herb flavors. Serve this with Greek Salad with Fried Leeks (page 107) and Spinach Phyllo Pie (page 87).

6 thinly cut lamb shoulder chops (about 4 pounds)

Coarse salt and freshly ground black pepper

¼ cup extra virgin olive oil, plus more for drizzling

Grated zest and juice of 1 lemon

3 garlic cloves, minced

2 tablespoons minced fresh mint

1 tablespoon minced fresh oregano

1 Preheat the broiler. Season the chops with salt and pepper. Broil chops, turning once, for 3½ minutes on each side, until they're medium pink in the center. Transfer to a platter.

2 Whisk together the remaining ingredients and pour over the chops. Let stand for a few minutes. Drizzle with olive oil before serving. *

SHOULDER CHOPS

Shoulder chops, both lamb and pork, are not to be overlooked. Marbled with rivulets of flavor and texture, they're significantly less expensive than precious loin chops. I like their texture and flavor. They are thin-cut and wide, like a pancake—not tall and lean!

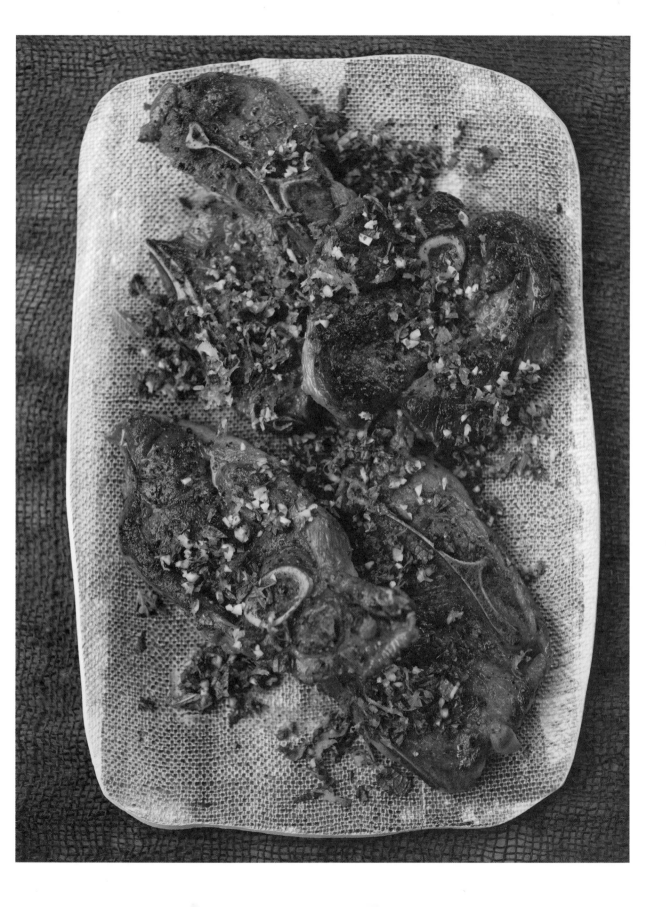

brined and fried chicken

serves 4

While I prefer thighs fried, it's hard to resist the moist and crispy breasts in this killer recipe. Brining meat, especially poultry, keeps the flesh moist and flavorful. Nowhere does this apply more than with white-meat fried chicken. The cornmeal in the "double dip" batter adds interesting texture and crunch and the hot pepper flakes give just enough kick to keep you on your toes.

BRINE

2 quarts cold water

⅔ cup coarse salt

⅓ cup sugar

⅓ cup molasses

8 thyme sprigs

2 bay leaves

One 3½-pound chicken, cut into 10 serving pieces

⅔ cup all-purpose flour

⅔ cup fine cornmeal

½ teaspoon coarse salt

1 teaspoon red pepper flakes

4 large eggs

3 quarts vegetable oil for deep-frying

NOTE The oil will drop to 300°F when the chicken is added. That is the correct temperature for frying the chicken. Bring the oil back up to 350°F before adding the second batch.

Customize the Brine Use the ratio of 2 quarts water and ⅔ cup each salt and sweetener as a base. You can alter the sweet to suit your own taste: honey, agave, barley malt, and mirin are good options. Partner the spices to complement the meat.

1 For the brine, combine 1 cup of the water, the salt, sugar, molasses, thyme, and bay leaves in a small saucepan and stir over medium heat just until the salt and sugar are dissolved. Remove from the heat and let cool.

2 Combine the brine mixture with the remaining 7 cups cold water in a large bowl or deep baking dish. Add the chicken, making sure it is covered with the brining liquid. Refrigerate for at least 8 hours, or up to 24 hours.

3 Set a cooling rack on a rimmed baking sheet. Remove the chicken from the brining liquid (discard the liquid) and pat dry. Combine the flour, cornmeal, salt, and red pepper flakes in a shallow dish. Whisk the eggs in another shallow dish. Coat the chicken in the flour mixture, then in the eggs, and again in the flour mixture; transfer to the baking sheet.

4 Heat the oil to 350°F in a large deep pot. If you intend to serve the chicken hot, preheat the oven to warm. Working in 2 batches, fry the chicken breasts for 15 minutes, turning once; the legs and thighs will take an additional 5 minutes. When done, the chicken pieces should be a deep golden brown (see Note). Transfer to a paper-towel-lined plate to drain. If desired, keep the first batch in the warm oven while you fry the rest. Serve hot or cold. ∗

chicken tikka masala

serves 6

Chicken tikka masala, the most famous of all Indian dishes, constitutes a whole food genre all its own. In fact, it's so popular in Britain that it's often called the country's national dish. This recipe takes inspiration from several traditional dishes and turns it all into one delicious hybrid. For a complete Indian feast, serve with Vegetable Biryani (page 203), a bowl of cool thick yogurt, some store-bought mango chutney, and Indian naan bread. **PHOTO ON PAGES 172–73**

12 boneless, skinless chicken thighs

Coarse salt and freshly ground black pepper

2 tablespoons safflower oil

1 small onion, chopped

3 garlic cloves, minced

One 1-inch piece ginger, peeled and finely grated

1 small green chili, such as serrano

1 tablespoon ground cumin

¼ teaspoon cayenne pepper

2 tablespoons garam masala

One 28-ounce can tomato puree

½ cup water

¼ cup heavy cream

1 Season the chicken with salt and pepper. Heat a large skillet over medium-high heat. Add the oil (see Note). When it shimmers, add the chicken to the hot pan and brown on both sides for about 3 minutes. (Work in batches if necessary.)

2 Transfer the chicken to a plate, and add the onions, garlic, and ginger to the pan. Cut a slit into the chili lengthwise and add to the pan. Sauté until the onions and garlic are softened, 3 to 5 minutes. Add the cumin, cayenne, and garam masala and cook for 30 seconds.

3 Add the tomato puree and water and stir. Add the chicken and bring to a simmer, then cover and simmer, turning the chicken occasionally, until it is cooked through and the sauce has thickened, about 30 minutes. (The dish can be made ahead to this point.)

4 Stir in the cream and simmer for 1 minute. Serve. ✴

NOTE Many cooks heat the oil and the pan together. When you start heating oil in a cold pan, it reaches the desired temperature slowly. That can increase the chance of scorching. Also, the longer the oil spends on the flame, the more likely it is to become a little gummy—and that means the food may stick to the pan. To avoid these situations, and because it gives me more control, I always heat my pan first and then add the oil.

OVERLEAF: Chicken Tikka Masala (above) and Vegetable Biryani (page 203), with breads, yogurt, and condiments for an Indian meal.

sesame chicken

serves 4

The thick crust and cloyingly sweet flavor of the typical take-out version of this dish turns me off. My kids disagree, brainwashed as they are by our local Chinese restaurant. But they also love this recipe. Skip the deep fryer and the thick batter, add some vegetables, and keep that delicious sesame umami-filled flavor. **PHOTO ON PAGES 18–19**

¼ cup soy sauce

2 tablespoons Chinese cooking wine (Shaoxing) or sherry

2 teaspoons cornstarch

1 teaspoon sugar

¼ teaspoon freshly ground black pepper

1 pound boneless, skinless chicken thighs, sliced into ½-inch-wide strips

2 tablespoons peanut oil

4 garlic cloves, minced

2 tablespoons minced peeled ginger

1 teaspoon Chinese chili paste

6 ounces snow peas, trimmed

One 8-ounce can bamboo shoots, drained and rinsed

One 8-ounce can water chestnuts, drained, rinsed, and halved

3 scallions, thinly sliced on the bias

3 tablespoons sesame seeds, toasted (see page 17)

2 teaspoons Asian sesame oil

1 Combine the soy sauce, wine, cornstarch, sugar, and pepper in a large bowl. Stir in the chicken and marinate for 15 minutes.

2 Place a wok or a heavy skillet over high heat. When it smokes, add the peanut oil. When the oil shimmers, add the garlic and ginger and stir-fry for 10 seconds. Remove the chicken from the marinade, reserving the marinade, and add to the wok. Stir-fry, stirring occasionally, until the chicken is browned in places and just cooked through, about 3 minutes.

3 Stir in the chili paste and snow peas and stir-fry for 2 minutes, or until the snow peas are shiny and bright green. Stir in the bamboo shoots and water chestnuts and stir-fry until heated through, about 1 minute.

4 Remove from the heat, stir in the scallions, sesame seeds, and sesame oil, and serve immediately. *

GOOD TO KNOW

Skillets If you cook for a large group regularly, buy a large cast-iron or stainless-steel skillet, preferably 14 inches. It will permit you to brown all the pieces of a 3- to 4-pound chicken in a single batch.

WOK COOKING

A good wok cannot be beat. Ours (over thirty years old) is made of uncoated carbon steel; one can be purchased today for as little as $20. There are a couple of things to keep in mind for wok cooking:

- Don't be afraid of using really high heat—that's how restaurant chefs do it.

- Cook in batches if you're cooking for a group: too much food in the wok will create steam instead of giving you the quick caramelize-frying you're looking for.

- I have a gas stove, and I dispense with the wok ring and put the pan directly on the burner.

- Have a good long-handled cooking spatula in hand to keep the food moving around in the wok, and don't walk away from it.

- You need to be thoroughly prepared, with all the meat and vegetables cut up and sauces, etc., within reach, before you start cooking.

If you don't have a wok, just use your largest skillet—preferably nonstick—and get it very hot before you start to cook. Use a little more oil and stir constantly when adding the onions and garlic to prevent burning them. (One of the benefits of a wok, with its round bottom, is that the oil will pool and cover the aromatics as they begin sizzling.)

chicken livornese

serves 4 to 6

Any chicken dish with Italian flavors that slowly simmers in the oven is my kind of dinner. As this stew bubbles away, the scent permeates the house with an irresistible aroma—and provides sense memories that will stay with your children for the rest of their lives. To get 18 pieces of chicken, cut each of the drumsticks, thighs, and wings in half and each of the breasts in thirds (or have your butcher do it). Serve with Creamy Polenta (page 204) to soak up the savory sauce.

One 4-pound chicken, cut into 18 pieces

1 teaspoon coarse salt

Freshly ground black pepper

2 tablespoons extra virgin olive oil

1 small yellow onion, chopped

2 garlic cloves, minced

1 tablespoon tomato paste

⅛ teaspoon red pepper flakes

¾ cup white wine

One 14½-ounce can whole plum tomatoes

½ cup Gaeta olives, pitted

1 rounded tablespoon salt-packed capers, rinsed and chopped

⅓ cup chopped fresh flat-leaf parsley

1 Preheat the oven to 375°F with a rack in the middle position. Season the chicken with the salt and some pepper.

2 Heat a 12-inch braiser pan or ovenproof skillet over medium-high heat. Add the oil. When it shimmers, working in batches, brown the chicken on both sides, starting skin side down, 3 to 4 minutes per side. Transfer to a plate.

3 Add the onions and garlic to the pan and sauté until translucent, about 3 minutes. Stir in the tomato paste and red pepper flakes and cook for 1 minute. Add the white wine, stirring to deglaze the pan, and boil to reduce the liquid by half. Stir in the tomatoes, olives, and capers.

4 Return the chicken to the pan, skin side up, and transfer to the oven. Braise for 35 minutes, or until an instant-read thermometer inserted into the center of the thickest piece of chicken registers 165°F. Sprinkle the parsley over the top and serve. ✷

GOOD TO KNOW

This dish can also braise away, partially covered, on the stovetop, on a portable burner, or in an electric skillet (about 10 minutes longer) at low heat if you don't feel like turning on the oven—or you don't have one. Oven heat, however, which surrounds the pan, just makes for more even cooking.

fried lake fish

serves 4

Mine was a youth spent in Windsor, Ontario, on the Detroit River, smack-dab in the middle of the Great Lakes, with their myriad lake fish: walleye pike, perch, lake trout, largemouth bass. If you weren't out on your boat catching the fish yourself, you were at a roadhouse scarfing down fried fillets and spinning the lazy Susan around to bring your favorite relish within reach.

Those roadhouses constitute my first restaurant memories: rollicking joints where families and laughing children shared the room with beer-drinking buddies. Perch and walleye pike are staple fish of Midwestern roadhouses, but you can use any thin, firm, white fish fillets.

Four 6-ounce pike or perch fillets	**1** Season the fish fillets with the salt and pepper and dust with the flour.
1 teaspoon coarse salt	
¼ teaspoon freshly ground black pepper	**2** Heat a large nonstick skillet over medium-high heat. Add the butter and oil and swirl them around. Place the fish skin side down in the skillet and cook until the skin is crispy and brown, about 4 minutes. Gently turn the fish and continue cooking just until the fillets are cooked through and the fish flakes when pierced with the tines of a fork, 3 to 4 minutes more.
¼ cup Wondra (superfine) flour	
2 tablespoons unsalted butter	
2 tablespoons extra virgin olive oil	
1 lemon, cut into wedges	
Old-Fashioned Relish Platter (page 239)	
	3 Transfer the fish to serving plates, garnish with the lemon wedges, and serve immediately, with the relish platter. ∗

HOW TO
PULL
IT OFF

Panfry Success Start with tempered fish: in spite of popular wisdom, fish should be at room temperature when cooked, just like meat. So give it 10 minutes out of the fridge or cooler before frying. Then, when it hits the hot pan, it will head straight to golden crispy instead of steaming as it comes up to temperature. All you need is some superfine flour (Wondra), seasoning, and the hot fat sizzling in the pan—the butter brings flavor, but the oil heats to the higher temperature necessary for that golden patina. For crispy skin, start skin side down, then flip. If necessary, add more butter or oil and flip again.

OPPOSITE: Fried Lake Fish (above) and Old-Fashioned Relish Platter (page 239)

steamed salmon with green mayonnaise

serves 4

This is a gentle and delicious way to cook salmon, unlike pan-searing, which is more likely to highlight the salmon oil flavor. You don't need a fish poacher or special poaching liquid to yield a flavorful piece of steamed salmon. Just start with the freshest-possible fish and take care not to overcook it.

One 1-pound fillet wild salmon

Coarse salt and ground white pepper

1 cup mayonnaise

Grated zest and juice of 1 lemon

1 scallion, finely chopped

1 tablespoon salt-packed capers, rinsed and chopped

1 tablespoon chopped fresh dill or dried dill

1 tablespoon finely chopped fresh parsley

1 Preheat the oven to 375°F with a rack in the upper third position. Season the salmon with the salt and white pepper. Place on a large piece of foil and close to make a loose-fitting, tightly sealed package.

2 Put the salmon on a baking sheet and cook for 20 to 25 minutes, until the fish is still slightly rare in the center (it should be only slightly resistant to the touch). Carefully open the foil and let the fish rest for a few minutes. Or let cool completely and chill before serving.

3 Meanwhile, combine the mayonnaise, lemon zest and juice, scallion, capers, dill, and parsley. Season to taste with salt.

4 Cut the fish into 4 pieces and serve with a dollop of sauce on the side. *

WILD ALASKAN SALMON

If there is one cooked fish front and center in a gourmet shop cold case, it's poached salmon. A precious wild food source, it's to be supported, respected, and cherished. Most U.S. wild salmon comes fresh out of Alaskan waters from June to September. Although fresh is best, flash-frozen at sea is superior to the farmed option any day. You'll pay for it, but wild fish is worth the trade-off for me. I'd rather eat it less often and have the best-tasting, best-for-the-environment choice. I'd rather eat canned wild Alaskan salmon than fresh farmed.

malaysian-style mussels

serves 4

This recipe was inspired by our local Belgian beer place, which has several different versions of *moules frites* on the menu: an enamel pot of mussels comes with a cone filled with crispy French fries and a mayonnaise dipping sauce alongside. My favorite is the Malaysian style, which is a riff on laksa, a coconut curry soup with Chinese-Malay elements. At home, mussels take literally minutes to prepare and need only a crispy baguette to sop up all the delicious juices.

2 tablespoons safflower oil

2 garlic cloves, minced

One ½-inch piece ginger, peeled and minced

1 tablespoon Thai red curry paste

1 cup unsweetened coconut milk

2 pounds mussels, scrubbed clean and beards removed

12 cilantro sprigs

1 lime, cut into wedges

1 Heat a large deep skillet over medium-high heat. Add the oil. When it shimmers, add the garlic and ginger and sauté until fragrant, about 1 minute. Stir in the curry paste and cook for 1 minute. Add the coconut milk and bring to a boil.

2 Add the mussels to the skillet, cover, and cook just until they open, 2 to 3 minutes. With a slotted spoon, transfer them to a serving bowl. (Discard any unopened mussels.) Pour the sauce over the mussels, garnish with the cilantro and lime, and serve immediately. Put out a bowl for the shells. *

HOW TO
PULL
IT OFF

Cleaning Mussels and Other Bivalves Most of the work for a dish like this is getting the shellfish cleaned, devoid of any grit or seaweed. I scrub each shell under cold running water, then soak them in a bowl of cold water for a few minutes. (Invest in a small kitchen scrub brush and reserve it for this task.) Lift them out, scrub again, and soak in fresh water; repeat the process until they are clean. Mussels have a "beard" that needs to be pulled out from the edge of the shell. Rope mussels—i.e., farmed—are one of the few cultivated seafood products I like. They are uniform in size and come clean, requiring much less work than their wild cousins to be ready for the pot.

CHAPTER SIX

NOODLES, RICE, AND CORN

OPPOSITE: Campanelle with Fresh Tomatoes, Arugula, and Peas (page 186)

campanelle with fresh tomatoes, arugula, and peas

serves 4

On many spring and summer nights, I want to eat the freshest vegetables possible with a minimal amount of cooking. This is an update of a pasta salad with barely wilted vegetables. A quick stop at the greengrocer, and you can make the sauce in the time it takes to boil water and cook the pasta. Use a wooden spoon or a large fork to crush the tomatoes. **PHOTO ON PAGE 184**

⅓ cup extra virgin olive oil

2 garlic cloves, smashed and peeled

1 pint grape tomatoes, crushed

Leaves from 3 basil sprigs, torn

1 teaspoon coarse salt

1 pound campanelle pasta

1 cup fresh or thawed frozen peas

3 cups baby arugula, roughly chopped

Shaved Parmesan cheese for garnish

1 Combine the olive oil, garlic, tomatoes, basil, and salt in a large serving bowl.

2 Cook the pasta in a large pot of boiling salted water until al dente, adding the peas for the last minute of cooking. Drain the pasta.

3 Remove the garlic cloves from the tomato mixture, if desired. Toss the pasta into the tomato mixture, along with the arugula. Garnish with Parmesan shavings. ＊

PASTA SHAPES

Pasta may be the most popular Italian contribution to the food world. Aside from the ubiquitous spaghetti noodles, there are hundreds of shapes, and each one is aerodynamically designed to match its intended sauce. Here are a few of the kinds of pasta I recommend using in these recipes:

- **Bucatini**
  The hollow center of this thick long pasta distinguishes it from spaghetti. It's my choice for a ragu such as Pasta with Sausage Meat Sauce (page 150).

- **Campanelle**
  The word campanelle means "little bells" in Italian. It's perfect for collecting all kinds of tasty morsels, such as the peas that snuggle inside the small cones with ruffled edges in Campanelle with Fresh Tomatoes, Arugula, and Peas (opposite).

- **Conchiglie**
  These small shells are great for soups and stews. In Ceci e Pasta (page 91), they mingle with the chickpeas in a pool of tomato sauce and invariably some of the chickpeas nest inside the shell.

- **Fettuccine**
  One of Italy's oldest and most common noodles, these ribbon-like strands cling to the hearty cream sauce in the Chicken Fettuccine Alfredo (page 190).

- **Fusilli**
  The twisted corkscrew shape catches the thick pesto in all its folds here in Spinach Pesto Fusilli (page 189).

spinach pesto fusilli

serves 4 to 6

The allure of store-bought pesto, embellished with weird ingredients and preservatives, is a mystery to me. It's an uncomplicated sauce made with a few ingredients in a food processor! Use it in or on all sorts of things, from sandwiches, to pasta sauce, from soup to a dressing for vegetables. My version, which uses spinach rather than the traditional basil, is a clever way to eat veggies— in a healthy sauce that clings to the insides of corkscrew-shaped fusilli. You can make the pesto a couple of hours in advance.

8 ounces baby spinach

¾ cup pine nuts, toasted (see Note), plus more for garnish

2 garlic cloves, smashed and peeled

½ cup grated Parmesan cheese, plus more for garnish

Grated zest and juice of 1 lemon

½ teaspoon coarse salt

¼ teaspoon freshly ground black pepper

½ cup extra virgin olive oil, plus more for serving

1 pound fusilli

1 Put half the spinach in a food processor and pulse until coarsely chopped. Add the remaining spinach and pulse to chop. Add the pine nuts, garlic, Parmesan, lemon zest and juice, salt, and pepper and puree.

2 With the motor running, slowly add the olive oil in a steady stream. Transfer the pesto to a large bowl. (If making in advance, lightly coat the pesto with olive oil and cover with plastic wrap. Refrigerate until ready to serve.)

3 Cook the pasta in a large pot of boiling salted water until al dente. Drain and toss with the pesto. Garnish with Parmesan cheese and toasted pine nuts. *

NOTE To toast pine nuts, preheat the oven to 350°F. Spread the nuts out on a baking sheet in a single layer and put in the oven for 10 minutes, shaking the sheet several times. (You can also do this in a toaster oven.)

GOOD TO KNOW Personalize Your Pesto The cheese, herb, and nut choices can all be changed to create different flavors. Just swap in equal parts of each ingredient; the garlic, olive oil, salt, and pepper remain the same.

- **Greens:** basil, cilantro, parsley, chervil, arugula, or watercress.
- **Nuts:** walnuts, hazelnuts, pecans, or macadamias.
- **Cheese:** Romano, Asiago, grana padana, or even Cotija.

chicken fettuccine alfredo

serves 4

Seemingly out of the blue while lazing on the couch, my son Luca asked me to make this for dinner one day. It was easy to trace his craving to a TV commercial for an "endless pasta bowl." I admit it—the commercial did make it look delicious. And, once again, we proved that homemade can be just as good as—if not better than—what you see in the ethereal world of television advertising. Only a young athlete could handle the calorie intake of this butter- and cream-laden dish.

1 pound boneless, skinless chicken breasts

Coarse salt and white pepper

2 tablespoons unsalted butter

4 garlic cloves

2 cups heavy cream

1 pound fettuccine

¾ cup grated Parmesan cheese, plus more for serving

1 Cut the chicken into 1-inch-wide strips. Season with salt and white pepper. Melt the butter in a 12-inch skillet over medium-high heat. Add the chicken and sauté until cooked through, about 8 minutes.

2 Meanwhile, simmer the garlic cloves in the cream in a saucepan for 10 minutes.

3 Cook the pasta in a large pot of boiling salted water until al dente.

4 Pour the cream into the pan with the chicken, removing the garlic cloves. Stir in the Parmesan.

5 Toss the pasta with the sauce and serve with extra Parmesan. ∗

GOOD TO KNOW

How to Cut Up a Whole Chicken Using kitchen shears, cut along both sides of the backbone to remove it (there's a spot in the joint where the sharp point of the shears will slide through easily). With a boning knife, remove the wings from the breast by cutting through the center of the bone between drumlet and breast. Separate the drumstick from the thigh and the thigh from the breast. Cut through the center of the chicken breast, through the bone and cartilage to separate the breast into two pieces.

BONELESS CHICKEN THIGHS

You can also use boneless thighs here—they offer the convenience of chicken breasts but have a much richer, more layered flavor. This makes them an alternative whenever you want to save on cooking time without sacrificing flavor. They also tend to stay far moister than breasts, so they are an excellent choice for grilling.

"Dude, do we have bacon?"

WORKING WITH WHAT YOU HAVE

Recently Luca called from his friend Ethan's on a Sunday afternoon. They wanted to cook a pasta dish. He asked if I could tell him how to make spaghetti carbonara. "Do you have bacon?" I asked. "Dude, do we have bacon?" he relayed to Ethan. "No." Carbonara out then. "Got chicken breasts?" I asked. "No." Eventually cream was unearthed (milk could have done the job) and some cheese for alfredo. Luca's verdict? "Creamy-cheesy pasta. Mad good."

spinach zucchini lasagna

serves 8

This meatless lasagna will put to rest for life memories of gourmet deli vegetarian lasagnas with chunks of undercooked vegetables and no point of view. It matches its animal-kingdom counterpart stride for stride. And it is impossible to stop at just one square.

¼ cup extra virgin olive oil

1 small yellow onion, finely chopped

2 teaspoons coarse salt

2 pounds baby spinach

4 tablespoons unsalted butter

¼ cup all-purpose flour

1 quart whole milk

1 packed cup grated Parmesan cheese

¼ teaspoon freshly grated nutmeg

¼ teaspoon freshly ground black pepper

2 medium zucchini (about 1 pound), sliced lengthwise into ¼-inch-thick planks

8 ounces no-boil lasagna noodles

6 ounces mozzarella, shredded

⅓ packed cup grated Pecorino Romano cheese

1 Preheat the oven to 375°F with a rack in the middle position. Heat a large pot over medium-high heat. Add 1 tablespoon of the oil. When it shimmers, add the onions and ½ teaspoon of the salt and cook, stirring occasionally, until the onions are translucent, about 3 minutes.

2 Add the spinach, a few handfuls at a time, to the pot and cook, stirring frequently, until wilted, 3 to 5 minutes. Transfer the spinach to a mesh strainer set over a bowl and press against it with a wooden spoon to remove as much liquid as possible.

3 Melt the butter in a medium saucepan over high heat. Add the flour and cook, whisking constantly, until the roux is golden brown, 4 to 5 minutes. Add the milk, whisking, and continue whisking until the sauce begins to boil and thickens enough to coat the back of a spoon. Remove from the heat and stir in the Parmesan, 1 teaspoon salt, the nutmeg, and pepper. Cover with plastic wrap pressed against the surface.

4 Heat the remaining 3 tablespoons oil in a large skillet over medium-high heat. Working in batches, add the zucchini and cook, turning once, until golden brown on both sides, about 2 minutes per side. Transfer to a paper-towel-lined plate to drain, and sprinkle with the remaining ½ teaspoon salt.

5 To assemble: Spread 1 cup of the cream sauce over the bottom of a 9-by-13-inch baking dish. Arrange one-third of the noodles over the sauce in a single overlapping layer. Top with 1 cup sauce and half of the spinach. Repeat with a second layer of noodles, sauce, and spinach. Top with the remaining noodles, remaining sauce, zucchini, mozzarella, and Pecorino.

6 Cover the baking dish with foil and bake for 45 minutes. Remove the foil and continue baking for about 15 minutes longer, until the cheese is golden in places and the lasagna is bubbling around the edges. Remove from the oven and let stand for 20 minutes before slicing and serving. *

LASAGNA NOODLES

No-boil noodles are convenient but not essential for this recipe. If using old-fashioned noodles
(or homemade), boil them in a large pot of salted water until tender but still firm. Drain, toss with
a little olive oil, and lay them out on a baking sheet, using parchment between each layer, until
ready to use. If prepping in advance, let cool, then cover with plastic wrap.

mac 'n' cheese

serves 6

Snap out of it, folks, and come back to homemade macaroni and cheese: old-school mac 'n' cheese, the kind our moms or grandmas made from scratch with a few humble ingredients. A tray of this crunchy-topped, gooey goodness—assembled and baked in under an hour—will be a revelation. Serve it with a salad as a whole (vegetarian) meal or as one of the Southern-style "meat-and-two" choices alongside Brined and Fried Chicken (page 170) and Collard Greens with Ham and Bacon (page 225).

1 pound elbow macaroni (or any pasta shape)

4 tablespoons unsalted butter

¼ cup all-purpose flour

1 quart whole milk

12 ounces cheese (cheddar, Munster, Monterey Jack—whatever you have in the fridge), shredded

¼ teaspoon freshly ground black pepper

Pinch of cayenne pepper

TOPPING

1½ cups panko bread crumbs, or homemade (see opposite)

2 tablespoons unsalted butter, melted

Hot sauce, such as Frank's Hot Red Sauce, for serving

1 Preheat the oven to 375°F with a rack in the middle position. Butter a 2½- to 3-quart baking dish.

2 Cook the pasta in a large pot of boiling salted water until al dente. Drain and return to the pot.

3 While the pasta cooks, melt the 4 tablespoons butter in a large saucepan over medium-high heat. Whisk in the flour and cook, whisking constantly, until the roux is golden and fragrant, about 2 minutes. Whisk in the milk, bring to a boil, and boil, whisking constantly, until thickened, about 5 minutes. Remove from the heat and add the cheese gradually, stirring until smooth; add the black pepper and cayenne with the last of the cheese. Pour the cheese sauce over the pasta and stir to combine. Transfer to the prepared baking dish.

4 To make the topping, combine the panko with the melted butter in a small bowl. Sprinkle over the macaroni and cheese and bake for 18 to 20 minutes, until golden on top.

5 Serve with the hot sauce. ∗

IMPROVISE & INFLUENCE

My son Calder says one of the most vivid kitchen memories of his childhood is a last-minute, scrounge-whatever's-in-the-house-'cause-we're-starving supper. ● It was before he knew how to cook, and I cleverly got him excited about not ordering in pizza. Instead, we rummaged through the fridge and pulled out literally ten different nubs of cheese. I showed him how to make a quick roux, boiled some pasta, grated the smorgasbord of cheeses, and made a mornay sauce, then put everything in a baking dish, topped it with bread crumbs, and slid it into the oven. Twenty minutes later, a delicious dinner came out, all the better for the manner in which it had been prepared.

shrimp pad thai

serves 4

Pad thai, right at the top of any Thai menu's noodle section, is everyone's favorite, with its sweet, salty, sour, and hot flavors—plus the "cold flavor" from the crunchy bean sprouts. My son Calder says that whenever you try a new Thai take-out place, you've got to order the pad thai as a barometer of the spot. Embrace the unusual ingredients here. Learn about Asian pantry items (see page 16) and you can replicate the best versions of your favorite dishes at home over and over.

8 ounces flat rice noodles

¾ cup tamarind juice
(see page 20)

¼ cup soy sauce

⅓ cup chopped palm sugar or ⅓ cup packed
light brown sugar

¼ cup plus 2 tablespoons fish sauce

1 teaspoon hot sauce, such as Sriracha,
plus more for serving

½ teaspoon safflower oil

3 shallots, thinly sliced

5 scallions, cut into 2-inch pieces,
bulbs halved lengthwise

1 pound medium shrimp, peeled and deveined

4 ounces fried tofu (see page 20),
thinly sliced

4 large eggs, lightly beaten

Garnishes: lime wedges, cilantro sprigs,
bean sprouts, unsalted roasted peanuts

1 Soak the noodles in a bowl of warm water for 30 minutes. Drain in a colander and cover with damp paper towels until ready to use.

2 Combine the tamarind juice, soy sauce, palm sugar, fish sauce, and hot sauce in a small saucepan and bring to a boil, stirring until the sugar is dissolved. Remove from the heat and set the sauce aside.

3 Heat a wok or a large skillet over medium-high heat. Add the oil (see Note, page 171). When it shimmers, carefully add half of the shallots and stir-fry until golden brown. Transfer to a paper-towel-lined plate to drain.

4 Raise the heat to high, add the remaining shallots, the scallions, and shrimp, and stir-fry just until the shrimp are opaque and firm to the touch, about 2 minutes. Using a slotted spoon, transfer to a plate. Add the tofu to the wok and heat through, about 1 minute. Transfer to the plate with the shrimp.

5 Add the eggs to the wok and cook, stirring constantly, just until set but still wet, about 1 minute. Transfer to the plate with the shrimp and tofu.

6 Add the sauce to the wok and bring to a boil. Stir in the noodles and stir-fry until hot, about 2 minutes. Return the scallions, shrimp, tofu, and eggs to the wok and stir to combine. Serve immediately with the garnishes and hot sauce. ⋆

BEAN SPROUTS

I grew up in a central-casting white-bread suburb, where Chinese takeout was considered kind of exotic. Mung bean sprouts were featured in many of the dishes. (Did you know cellophane noodles are made from the starch extracted from mung bean sprouts?) They make a great side dish.

NUTSHELL RECIPE: bean sprouts two ways

Sauté 3 cups sprouts over high heat with 1 tablespoon minced ginger and 2 cloves minced garlic. Or toss fresh sprouts in a dressing of equal parts vinegar and soy sauce, ¼ teaspoon sesame oil, and a pinch of sugar—superb on a chilled salad.

cold soba noodles with dipping sauce

serves 6

I can think of few dishes more appealing on a hot summer day than cold buckwheat (soba) noodles with a dipping sauce. Buckwheat is an entirely different grain from wheat, and it is full of protein. For a complete Japanese menu, serve with Pork Tonkatsu (page 161) and Japanese Shredded Cabbage (page 237). Because buckwheat is gluten-free, this dish is easily adaptable for those with gluten intolerances—simply substitute wheat-free tamari for the soy sauce.

3 tablespoons safflower or peanut oil

1 large shallot, halved lengthwise and thinly sliced crosswise (⅓ cup)

3½ ounces bunashimeji (beech mushrooms) or button mushrooms, sliced

9 ounces soba noodles

¼ cup plus 2 tablespoons soy sauce or tamari

¼ cup rice wine vinegar

1 teaspoon hot sauce, such as Sriracha

2 teaspoons Asian sesame oil

2 scallions, thinly sliced on the bias

½ English cucumber, cut into 1½-inch-long matchsticks

2 tablespoons sesame seeds, toasted (see page 17)

1 Heat a large skillet over medium-high heat. Add 2 tablespoons of the oil. When it shimmers, add the shallots and mushrooms and sauté until the shallots are golden and the mushrooms brown in places, 3 to 4 minutes. Transfer to a large bowl.

2 Bring a large pot of water to a boil and cook the noodles according to the package instructions. Drain. Toss the noodles with the shallots, mushrooms, and the remaining tablespoon of oil. Let cool to room temperature.

3 Whisk together the soy sauce, rice wine vinegar, hot sauce, sesame oil, and scallions in a medium bowl. Divide the dipping sauce among individual serving bowls.

4 Toss the cucumber and sesame seeds with the noodles and serve with the dipping sauce. ∗

COLD NOODLES

Chilled noodles are often served in the summer in Japanese restaurants, so why not try some at home? Wheat noodles such as ramen (thin) or udon (thick and chewy) as well as soba (buckwheat) noodles are available in the international section of your market or online (see page 16). Cook the noodles as directed, drain, and toss them in a little oil to separate before putting in the fridge to chill. Serve cold noodles with whatever you have on hand—don't be afraid to improvise. Try fresh shredded vegetables such as carrots, cabbage, or daikon radish. Top with leftover cold sliced meat or poultry and a dipping sauce.

pork and ginger wonton stir-fry

serves 4

Put this dish in your family meal rotation right alongside the likes of spaghetti and meatballs—that's how much the fans will love it. This is an inside-out dumpling/noodle dish, a stir-fry of boiled wonton wrappers and the ingredients found in typical Chinese dumplings. If you order chow fun for Chinese takeout, it's the recipe for you.

8 ounces wontons skins

Salt

¼ cup soy sauce

2 tablespoons rice wine vinegar

½ teaspoon sugar

1 teaspoon cornstarch

2 tablespoons safflower or peanut oil

2 garlic cloves, minced

One 1-inch piece ginger, peeled and minced

1 pound ground pork

1 serrano chili, thinly sliced

3 scallions, thinly sliced

1 lime, cut into wedges

1. Separate the wonton skins so they do not stick together. Cut the wontons into thirds, so they resemble wide, short noodles. Set aside.

2. Put a large pot of salted water on to boil.

3. Stir together the soy sauce, rice wine vinegar, and sugar in a small bowl. Whisk in the cornstarch.

4. Heat a large skillet over medium-high heat. Add the oil. When it shimmers, add the garlic and ginger and cook until fragrant, about 1 minute. Add the ground pork, breaking it up with a spoon into smaller pieces, and cook until cooked through and no longer pink, 3 to 5 minutes.

5. When the pork is cooked, add the sauce mixture and cook until the liquid has been absorbed. Stir in 1 tablespoon salt and the sliced chilies and scallions.

6. Drop the wontons into the boiling water (you may need to separate them again as you add them to the pot—use your fingers). Stir and cook until they rise to the top and are tender, 1 to 2 minutes. Drain well and add to the pan with the pork.

7. Squeeze the lime juice over the dish and serve immediately. ∗

GROUND PORK

I keep plastic-wrapped 1-pound portions of ground pork, which defrosts quickly, in the freezer. Submerge the wrapped pork in hot water to thaw. You can also fry it straight from the freezer, stirring as it browns, in a hot pan with oil. Here are a few ideas for using ground pork:

- Make larb, the addictive Thai cold salad, flavored with lime, chili, and fish sauce and topped with crunchy peanuts.

- Add to the meat mix of chili (see page 156).

- Italian pasta sauces are as delicious with ground pork as with beef—or both.

- Make homemade breakfast sausages.

{ NUTSHELL RECIPE: **breakfast sausage** }
Mix ground pork with ground sage, dried thyme, minced garlic, salt, and black pepper, form into patties, and fry in oil until golden.

pork fried rice

serves 4

This is easily my husband's favorite Chinese take-out choice. Onions, pork, and scrambled eggs— greasy and satisfying. When you make it at home, you get the flavor of the Chinese joint but with fresher ingredients and minus the grease slick, thank you very much. **PHOTO ON PAGES 18–19**

12 ounces pork tenderloin, cut into ½-inch dice

2 tablespoons hoisin sauce

1 tablespoon honey

3 tablespoons soy sauce

¾ teaspoon Chinese five-spice powder

2 tablespoons peanut oil

½ large white onion, finely chopped

4 garlic cloves, minced

1 medium carrot, peeled and finely chopped

3 cups cooked white rice

4 large eggs, lightly beaten

½ cup frozen peas, thawed

3 scallions, thinly sliced on the bias

1 teaspoon Asian sesame oil

1 Combine the pork, hoisin, honey, soy sauce, and five-spice powder in a medium bowl. Marinate for 15 minutes.

2 Heat a wok over high heat. When the wok smokes, add the oil. When the oil shimmers, add the onions and garlic and cook, stirring, for 30 seconds. Drain the pork, reserving the marinade, add to the wok, and cook, stirring, until browned, 2 to 3 minutes.

3 Add the carrots and rice, along with the reserved marinade, and cook, stirring constantly, until the liquid has been absorbed, about 2 minutes.

4 Create a well in the center of the wok, pour in the eggs, and scramble. Add the peas, scallions, and sesame oil to the wok and stir until incorporated. Serve immediately. *

{ NUTSHELL RECIPE: **basic white rice**

Put 2 cups long-grain rice, 1½ teaspoons salt, and 3 cups water in a saucepan and stir briefly, just to distribute evenly. Over high heat, bring to a rolling boil; then reduce heat to low and simmer, covered, for 20 minutes. This recipe makes 2 quarts rice and leftovers freeze well. }

vegetable biryani

serves 6 to 8

I adore the spicy mystery of Indian food, but it doesn't really take much to match its complex essence at home. Biryani is a richly spiced, exotically flavored, rice dish; this version, full of vegetables and infused with spices and coconut milk, is ideal for vegetarians. It's a meal in itself, but I also love to serve it with Chicken Tikka Masala (page 171). Leftovers get a fried egg on top for breakfast. **PHOTO ON PAGE 173**

⅓ cup plus 2 tablespoons safflower oil

1 medium yellow onion, quartered

1½ teaspoons coarse salt

2 teaspoons cumin seeds

1 teaspoon coriander seeds

1 tablespoon poppy seeds

6 whole cloves

2 bay leaves

One 1-inch piece cinnamon stick

One 1½-inch piece ginger, peeled

¼ cup unsweetened shredded coconut

1 cup unsweetened coconut milk

2 cups basmati rice

2⅓ cups water

2 small russet (baking) potatoes, peeled and chopped

2 medium carrots, peeled and chopped

One 10-ounce package frozen peas

1 Combine ⅓ cup of the oil, the onion, salt, spices, ginger, coconut, and ¼ cup of the coconut milk in a blender and blend until smooth.

2 Heat a large straight-sided skillet with a tight-fitting lid over medium heat. Add the remaining 2 tablespoons oil. When it shimmers, add the rice and toast until lightly golden, about 2 minutes. Add the spice puree and cook, stirring, until aromatic, about 3 minutes.

3 Add the remaining ¾ cup coconut milk, the water, potatoes, and carrots and bring to a simmer, then cover and simmer until the water is absorbed, about 15 minutes.

4 Remove from the heat, add the peas, cover, and let steam until the peas are heated through, about 5 minutes. ✳

Recipe Ingredients Lists   Long ingredients lists can be a bit daunting. Frankly, that can be a big turnoff, so I always try to get the essence of an authentic dish with the fewest possible ingredients. But Indian cuisine is incredibly elaborate and richly nuanced, and sometimes you must embrace a little challenge to get an amazing result. I keep an airtight plastic tub in the pantry to house my Indian spices. Since I don't use them regularly, it keeps everything fresh. And having them on hand means I'm much more likely to take on a dish like this or to experiment with other Indian recipes from my cookbook collection.

creamy polenta

serves 6 to 8

Polenta is a great carb-starch to match with saucy Italian foods. Here, served soft and loose, it makes a great accompaniment to Chicken Livornese (page 176).

4 cups water

1 tablespoon coarse salt

1 pound (2⅔ cups) quick-cooking polenta

4 ounces soft goat cheese

½ cup grated Parmesan cheese

2 tablespoons unsalted butter, at room temperature

1 Bring the water to a boil in a medium saucepan. Add the salt, then slowly add the polenta in a thin stream, whisking constantly to avoid lumps. Continue whisking until thick and creamy, about 5 minutes.

2 Stir in the cheeses and butter. Serve immediately, or use in the next recipe. ⋆

crispy polenta squares with cherry tomatoes

serves 4 to 6

Polenta can simply be allowed to firm up, be cut into pieces, and then be baked until crisp, as described below, to accompany any Italian dish. But this juicy cherry tomato topping makes it a light lunch or snack on its own.

½ recipe Creamy Polenta (opposite), just made (see Note)

Extra virgin olive oil

TOPPING

1 pint grape tomatoes, halved

2 tablespoons extra virgin olive oil

½ teaspoon coarse salt

¼ teaspoon freshly ground black pepper

1 teaspoon chopped fresh thyme

1 Pour the warm polenta into an oiled 8-inch square pan and smooth the top. Refrigerate until firm, at least 2 hours, or as long as overnight.

2 Preheat the oven to 450°F with a rack in the upper third position. Flip the polenta onto a cutting board. Brush the top with olive oil. Cut into sixteen 2-inch squares.

3 Preheat a baking sheet in the oven for a few minutes, then place the squares on the sheet. Bake for 10 minutes.

4 Meanwhile, make the tomato topping: combine all the ingredients in a bowl, tossing to coat the tomatoes.

5 Increase the oven setting to broil and cook until the polenta squares are golden brown on top, about 3 minutes. Transfer to a platter, scatter the tomato mixture on top, and serve. *

NOTE

No one should let the remaining half batch of Creamy Polenta go to waste; and of course you may have already eaten it! If not, firm it up as directed, then for breakfast, slice it and sauté in butter and serve with a fried egg on top. Any leftover slices can be wrapped in plastic wrap and frozen, to be used later individually.

chicken tamales with salsa roja

yields 12 tamales

Maria, a wizard tamale maker, sells delicious homemade cheese and chicken tamales from a cart next to the subway entrance close to my apartment. There is always a quick-moving line of folks buying her food (rice porridge and spiced hot chocolate too) before starting their day, and everything's sold out by 10 a.m. My kids get some before heading off to school (even if I've fed them at home) and my husband frequently picks up a bagful for his coworkers. Making tamales is labor-intensive, but that's what it's about: the love you put into it really comes out in the tastiness of the end result. If you want a similar flavor without the labor, try Tamale Pie (page 154).

15 dried corn husks

1 pound boneless, skinless chicken breasts (or use thighs)

8 ounces chicken broth, homemade (page 57) or store-bought

TAMALE DOUGH

2½ cups masa harina

8 ounces lard or unsalted butter, at room temperature

2½ teaspoons coarse salt

3 cups fresh corn kernels or frozen corn, thawed and thoroughly drained

½ cup plus 2 tablespoons warm chicken broth or water

1 teaspoon coarse salt

¼ teaspoon freshly ground black pepper

Salsa Roja (recipe follows)

1 Put 12 of the corn husks in a large bowl, cover with hot water, and weight down with a plate to keep them submerged. Soak until soft and pliable, about 2 hours; drain.

2 Poach the chicken in the chicken broth for 12 to 15 minutes, according to the directions on page 103. When it is cool enough to handle, shred it into small pieces.

3 To make the dough, combine the masa harina, lard, and salt in a food processor and pulse until the consistency of coarse cornmeal. Transfer to a large bowl.

4 Add 2 cups of the corn kernels to the processor bowl and puree; transfer to the bowl with the masa mixture. Stir in the remaining corn kernels and the chicken broth. Knead the mixture with your hands until a dough forms. Cover with a damp towel until ready to use.

5 Tear the remaining 3 corn husks into thin strips, to yield 24 strips. Season the chicken with the salt and pepper.

6 Place a corn husk on your flattened palm. Pinch off ⅓ cup of the dough with your other hand and press it onto the center of the husk to make a 4-by-3-inch rectangle. Press ¼ cup of the chicken into the center of the dough. Close your palm so the sides of the husk cover the dough and place on a work surface with a long side of the husk facing you. Roll up the husk into a tight log, fold the wider end of the husk over, and tie with a strip of corn husk. Twist the thinner end of the husk and tie with another corn husk strip (see photo, opposite). Repeat the process to form the remaining tamales.

7 Insert a steamer basket inside a large pot filled with 1 inch of water and bring the pot to a boil. Place the tamales in the basket, cover the pot, and steam for 1 hour, checking the pot occasionally and adding hot water as needed to prevent scorching.

8 Serve the tamales with the salsa. ⋆

salsa roja

makes 3 cups

Roasting the vegetables first is a superb way to make a deeply flavored salsa.

1½ pounds plum tomatoes, halved lengthwise

1 medium white onion, cut into 8 wedges

3 jalapeños, stems removed and halved

4 garlic cloves, peeled

2 tablespoons extra virgin olive oil

¼ cup coarsely chopped fresh cilantro

1½ teaspoons coarse salt

Juice of 1 lime

⅓ cup chicken broth

1 Preheat the oven to 450°F with a rack in the upper third position. Put the tomatoes, cut side up, on a rimmed baking sheet, along with the onions, 2 of the jalapeños, and the garlic. Drizzle with the oil and roast for 22 to 25 minutes, until the vegetables are blistered in places and wilting. Remove from the oven (see photo, pages 142–43).

2 Put the remaining jalapeño halves in a food processor, and pulse until finely chopped. Add the roasted vegetables and any accumulated juices, along with the cilantro, salt, lime juice, and chicken broth. Pulse until smooth.

3 The salsa can be stored in an airtight container in the refrigerator for up to 2 weeks. ⋆

cheese tamales with roasted salsa verde

makes 12 tamales

Cheese tamales have a gooey interior texture next to the soft steamed dough. It's interesting to offer a few different types of tamales at a party.

15 dried corn husks

2 large poblano peppers

Tamale Dough (page 207)

8 ounces Monterey Jack cheese, shredded

Roasted Salsa Verde (recipe follows)

1 Put 12 of the corn husks in a large bowl, cover with hot water, and weight down with a plate to keep them submerged. Soak until soft and pliable, about 2 hours; drain.

2 Put the poblanos directly over an open gas flame and char, turning with tongs, until blackened on all sides, about 5 minutes. Transfer to a plastic bag and let steam for 10 minutes.

3 Using a paper towel, rub the skin from the peppers. Remove the stems and seeds and coarsely chop the poblanos.

4 Tear the remaining 3 corn husks into thin strips, to yield 24 strips.

5 Place a corn husk on your flattened palm. Pinch off ⅓ cup of the dough with your other hand and press it onto the center of the husk to make a 4-by-3-inch rectangle. Press ¼ cup of the cheese and 2 tablespoons of the chopped poblanos into the center of the dough. Close your palm so the sides of the husk cover the dough and place on a work surface with a long side of the husk facing you. Roll up the husk into a tight log, fold the wider end of the husk over, and tie with a strip of corn husk. Twist the thinner end of the husk and tie with another corn husk strip (see photo, page 209). Repeat the process to form the remaining tamales.

6 Insert a steamer basket inside a large pot filled with 1 inch of water and bring the pot to a boil. Place the tamales in the basket, cover the pot, and steam for 1 hour, checking the pot occasionally and adding hot water as needed to prevent scorching.

7 Serve the tamales with the salsa. ✴

GOOD TO KNOW

Here's a trick to prevent scorching: Place a few coins in the water-filled pot. As long as the water level is correct, you'll hear the coins clinking away. If there's silence, it's time to add some more water.

roasted salsa verde

Makes 3 cups

This is similar to the classic green sauce served in Mexican restaurants.

1½ pounds tomatillos, husks removed and thoroughly washed and dried

½ medium white onion, quartered lengthwise and halved crosswise

2 jalapeños, stems removed

6 garlic cloves, peeled

½ cup coarsely chopped fresh cilantro

1¼ teaspoons coarse salt

½ teaspoon sugar

Juice of 1 lime

⅓ cup chicken broth

1 Heat a large cast-iron skillet over high heat. When the pan begins to smoke, add the tomatillos, onions, jalapeños, and garlic. Blister the vegetables, turning frequently, until blackened in places but still firm, about 5 minutes.

2 Transfer the vegetables to a food processor, add the cilantro, salt, and sugar, and pulse until the vegetables are very finely chopped. Transfer to a small saucepan and bring to a simmer over medium-high heat, then reduce the heat and simmer, stirring occasionally, until slightly thickened, about 10 minutes. Remove from the heat, stir in the lime juice and broth, and let cool to room temperature.

3 The salsa can be stored in an airtight container in the refrigerator for up to 2 weeks. ✶

CHAPTER SEVEN

VEGGIES
AND OTHER SIDES

OPPOSITE: Baked Potato Poppers (page 214)

baked potato poppers

makes 24 poppers; serves 6

These crispy potato puffs unabashedly copy, but far surpass, the commercial brand found in the frozen section of your supermarket. Baked rather than deep-fried, they are perfectly crispy on the outside and meltingly soft on the inside. They will fool even the most die-hard tater tot fiend. You can't stop eating them. Panko bread crumbs are essential to the dish's success, providing the crispiest crunch. **PHOTO ON PAGE 212**

2 large russet (baking) potatoes (about 1 pound)

½ cup all-purpose flour

1 tablespoon cornstarch

½ teaspoon coarse salt

¼ teaspoon white pepper

1 large egg yolk

1½ cups panko bread crumbs

¼ cup extra virgin olive oil

Ketchup

1 Preheat the oven to 425°F, with a rack in the middle position. Put a rimmed baking sheet in the oven to preheat. Peel and grate the potatoes, and transfer to a large bowl. Cover with boiling water by two inches. Let stand for 10 minutes.

2 Drain the potatoes in a colander and rinse thoroughly with cold water. Squeeze the potatoes to remove excess moisture, and transfer back to the large bowl. Add the flour, cornstarch, salt, pepper, and egg yolk and fold into the potatoes.

3 Spread the panko on another rimmed baking sheet. With wet hands, pinch off tablespoons of the potato mixture, form into balls, and coat with the panko crumbs.

4 Carefully remove the hot baking sheet from the oven and coat with 2 tablespoons of the olive oil. Quickly transfer the poppers to the baking sheet and drizzle with the remaining 2 tablespoons olive oil. Bake for about 30 minutes, flipping once, until golden brown and crispy. Serve with ketchup. *

roasted rosemary potatoes

serves 4 to 6

Oven-roasting is just about the easiest potato preparation you can do, and yet the results are so delicious you'll reap bushels of praise. These are a yummy alternative to mashed potatoes with Old-School Meat Loaf (page 152). Feel free to switch out the rosemary for oregano, thyme, sage, or another hearty herb, depending on what flavor complements the rest of your meal.

PHOTO ON PAGES 216–17

1 pound red new potatoes, washed and dried

3 rosemary sprigs

Extra virgin olive oil

Coarse salt and freshly ground black pepper

1 Preheat the oven to 400°F with a rack in the upper third position. Put the potatoes and rosemary on a rimmed baking sheet, drizzle with olive oil, and season with salt and pepper. Shake the pan to coat the potatoes.

2 Roast the potatoes for 30 to 40 minutes, until cooked through and slightly golden. ✳

creamy chive mashed potatoes

serves 6

The luscious creaminess comes from mascarpone cheese. Tossing chopped chives in at the end adds just a hint of onion flavor. Mashed potatoes are a universal comfort food that unites us all.

PHOTO ON PAGE 217

6 russet (baking) potatoes, peeled and halved

Salt

1 cup whole milk, warmed

4 ounces mascarpone cheese

¼ cup chopped fresh chives

1 Put the potatoes in a large pot and cover with cold water by 2 inches. Season generously with salt, bring to a boil, and cook until the potatoes are very tender, about 40 minutes.

2 Drain the potatoes and return to the pot. Using a potato masher or ricer, mash them with the warm milk until smooth. Fold in the mascarpone and chives, and season with 1 teaspoon salt. ✳

fingerling potato salad

serves 4 to 6

The trick for infusing flavor into potato salad is adding the dressing while the potatoes are hot. The warm potatoes suck the tangy flavor right in. Combined with capers, red onion, lemon, and parsley, this is a great all-around potato salad, warm or at room temperature. Use small red jacket potatoes if fingerlings are unavailable. **PHOTO ON PAGE 216**

2 pounds fingerling or small red jacket potatoes

½ cup extra virgin olive oil

1 garlic clove, smashed and peeled

¼ teaspoon red pepper flakes

1 tablespoon salt-packed capers, rinsed and coarsely chopped, or 1 tablespoon vinegar

½ medium red onion, chopped

1 celery stalk, thinly sliced on the bias

Grated zest and juice of 1 lemon

2 tablespoons chopped fresh parsley

Coarse salt

1 Put the potatoes in a medium saucepan and cover with water by 2 inches. Season generously with salt, bring to a boil, and cook until the potatoes are tender, about 10 minutes.

2 Meanwhile, combine the olive oil, garlic, red pepper flakes, capers, and red onion in a small saucepan and bring to a simmer. Remove from the heat.

3 Drain the potatoes, halve lengthwise, and toss with the warm dressing, celery, lemon zest and juice, and parsley in a large bowl. Season with salt and serve warm or at room temperature. ∗

Potato Options

- You can boil the potatoes without peeling them first; the peels will come off easily when they are hot.

- Or you can leave the peels on (which adds texture and nutrients), mash, and ignore. Be sure to scrub the potatoes before cooking.

- You can bake the potatoes instead of boiling them (see Loaded Potato Skins, page 123, for baking instructions). Then peel and mash.

- Instead of mashing, you can use a ricer, which gives a smoother texture.

OVERLEAF, CLOCKWISE FROM LEFT: Fingerling Potato Salad (above); Roasted Rosemary Potatoes (page 215); Creamy Chive Mashed Potatoes (page 215).

italian fries

serves 6 (if you are very lucky)

Easily one of the top three most-loved recipes for generations in my own family, these oven-baked fries have become a new standard for many friends and fans. Just the scent of them cooking in the oven will make folks in the vicinity salivate. Enrobed in tangy-savory Romano cheese and herbs, the potatoes soften while the cheese melts and browns to a tender-crisp perfection. This is a first-rate potato partner for any plate.

6 or 7 Idaho potatoes, peeled and sliced into ⅓-inch-thick French fry–style strips (see Note), soaked in cold salted water

4 tablespoons (¼ cup) extra-virgin olive oil

1 tablespoon dried Italian herbs or some combo of dried oregano, thyme, marjoram, and basil

2 cups freshly grated Romano cheese

¼ cup fresh parsley leaves, finely chopped

4 tablespoons (½ stick) salted butter, cut into 6 cubes

Coarse salt and freshly ground black pepper

1 Preheat the oven to 400°F.

2 Drain the potatoes and pat dry with paper towels. Spread 1 tablespoon of the olive oil on each of 2 rimmed baking sheets and spread out the potatoes. Overlapping is fine.

3 Sprinkle the dried herbs evenly over the potatoes. Liberally spread the cheese and parsley on top. Drizzle the remaining 2 tablespoons of olive oil over the cheese. Scatter the cubed butter around the pans.

4 Bake until the potatoes are golden brown, rotating the pans after 30 minutes, for 45 to 50 minutes total. Use a spatula to lift off the potatoes with all the crusty cheese adhered to them. Sprinkle with salt and pepper to taste. Serve hot. ∗

NOTE For a French-fry cut, peel the potatoes and slice lengthwise into ⅓-inch-thick slices. Stack the slices on top of one another, a few at a time, and slice lengthwise into ⅓-inch-thick strips. Peeled and sliced potatoes can turn brown pretty quickly. To avoid this, try floating the peeled, cut pieces in cold, salted water. When you're ready to cook, drain them and pat dry.

candied sweet potatoes

serves 6

These gorgeously orange tubers will satisfy your desire for something salty, silky, and sweet. They're as welcome on the Thanksgiving table as they are as a side in a soul food restaurant.

2 pounds sweet potatoes, peeled, halved crosswise, and cut into 1-inch-thick wedges

3 tablespoons unsalted butter

⅓ cup packed dark brown sugar

1½ teaspoons coarse salt

¼ teaspoon freshly ground black pepper

½ cup water

Combine the sweet potatoes, butter, brown sugar, salt, pepper, and water in a straight-sided 10-inch skillet with a tight-fitting lid, and bring to a boil over high heat, stirring the potatoes to coat with the liquid. Lower the heat, cover, and simmer undisturbed until the potatoes are tender but not mushy, 12 to 15 minutes. Uncover and continue cooking, stirring gently a few times, until most of the liquid has evaporated and the potatoes are caramelized, about 5 minutes more. *

braised green beans and chickpeas

serves 6

This hearty side is a warm riff on bean salad. Serve it alongside Spinach Zucchini Lasagna (page 192) for a vegetarian meal that will keep diehard meat eaters happy as well.

2 tablespoons extra virgin olive oil

1 large shallot, thinly sliced

½ teaspoon coarse salt

¼ teaspoon red pepper flakes

1 pound green beans, trimmed and washed, water left clinging to the beans

One 15½-ounce can chickpeas, drained and rinsed

1 basil sprig

½ lemon

1 Heat an 8-inch-wide pot over medium heat. Add the olive oil (see Note, page 171). When it shimmers, scatter in the shallots and sprinkle on the salt and red pepper flakes. Top with the green beans, cover, and cook over medium heat for 10 minutes.

2 Add the chickpeas and basil sprig, stir to combine, and cook for 10 minutes, until the beans are tender and the chickpeas are cooked through. Remove from the heat, squeeze the lemon over, and serve. *

shaved and steamed broccoli

serves 4

I've cooked endless heads of broccoli by separating the floret clumps and steaming them whole. But a simple alteration—shaving or thinly slicing the florets first—changes the texture and the experience of eating this vegetable. The key is to avoid overcooking the broccoli; steam it just enough to yield to the bite without sacrificing a pleasant chew.

1 bunch broccoli, florets separated and thinly sliced or shaved

Extra virgin olive oil

Coarse salt

¼ teaspoon red pepper flakes

1 Bring ¼ inch of water to a boil in a 3-quart saucepan. Add the broccoli to the pan, cover, and steam for 3 minutes, until al dente.

2 Using a slotted spoon, transfer the broccoli to a serving dish. Drizzle with olive oil, season with salt and the red pepper flakes, and toss to coat. ✳

SPRING FLING

sautéed asparagus with shaved parmesan

serves 6

A fresh, simple preparation that you'll find in a legit Italian trattoria during asparagus season, or displayed in a gourmet-counter food case any time of year.

2 tablespoons extra virgin olive oil

2 pounds asparagus, ends trimmed and cut on the bias into 2-inch pieces

1 teaspoon coarse salt

Rounded ¼ teaspoon freshly ground black pepper

1 teaspoon grated orange zest

Juice of 1 orange

3 ounces shaved Parmesan cheese to taste

1 Heat a large skillet over high heat. Add the oil. When it shimmers, add the asparagus, salt, and pepper and sauté, stirring frequently, until the asparagus is crisp-tender, about 3 minutes. Stir in the orange zest and cook for 1 minute. Add the orange juice and stir a few times.

2 Transfer to a serving platter and scatter the Parmesan over the top. Serve immediately. ✳

collard greens with ham and bacon

serves 6

Stewed collard greens are yum. Collard greens with bacon are really yum. And collard greens with bacon *and* ham are yummy to the max. Adding a smoked pork product to a dish is a very easy way to take its flavor profile to a whole other level; add two smoked pork products, and you take it to another stratosphere.

3 ounces (3 slices) bacon, cut into ½-inch pieces

1 small yellow onion, chopped

2 garlic cloves, minced

3 ounces smoked ham, cut into ½-inch pieces

2 cups chicken broth

2 pounds collard greens, stems and thick center ribs removed, leaves coarsely chopped

½ teaspoon coarse salt

1 Cook the bacon in a large pot over medium-high heat just until it renders its fat; it shouldn't become crispy. Add the onions and cook, stirring occasionally, until translucent, about 3 minutes. Add the garlic and ham and cook for 1 minute, until fragrant.

2 Add the chicken broth and bring to a boil, scraping up the brown bits from the bottom of the pot. Add the collard greens and salt and cook, uncovered, stirring occasionally, until the greens are tender and most of the liquid has evaporated, 25 to 30 minutes. ∗

COLLARD GREENS

A powerhouse vegetable, collards are a staple on Southern tables. Very "proteiny" for a green, they could be the steak impostor on a plate—they've got that much swagger. But collards talk the way they walk—loaded to the gills with vitamins, minerals, and fiber. They appear weekly on our table.

creamed spinach

serves 6

If there is one master recipe that hooked my kids on spinach, it's this one. Using the super simple but widely serviceable technique of béchamel sauce (see page 65) as a base, the lightly steamed spinach floats within a silky coating for a dreamy combination of texture and flavor. You'll make this one over and over.

2½ pounds fresh spinach, washed, water still clinging to the leaves

BÉCHAMEL SAUCE

3 tablespoons unsalted butter

¼ cup all-purpose flour

1 cup milk

1 teaspoon coarse salt

Pinch of freshly ground black pepper

Pinch of ground nutmeg

1 Steam the spinach in a large pot for 2 to 4 minutes, until the leaves have all collapsed. The water clinging to the leaves will be enough to cook it. Drain, cool, and squeeze out the liquid in a strainer. Coarsely chop the spinach.

2 To make the béchamel, heat a sauté pan over medium heat, and then melt the butter and whisk in the flour. Cook, stirring, for 1 minute. Whisk in the milk until fully incorporated and simmer for 30 seconds. Stir in the salt, pepper, and nutmeg.

3 Fold in the spinach and serve immediately. *

stir-fried watercress with garlic

serves 4

Watercress is usually eaten raw (or plopped on a restaurant plate in place of parsley to dress it up), but this Chinese-style preparation calls for cooking it in a wok over high heat. You can also use a large skillet, but the cooking must be hot and fast. It's all in the technique of adding ingredients gradually to build and layer flavors. Many greens can be cooked this way, like spinach, shredded cabbage, bok choy, and pea shoots. Serve with Sesame Chicken (page 174) and Pork Fried Rice (page 202). **PHOTO ON PAGES 18–19**

2 tablespoons soy sauce

1 tablespoon Chinese cooking wine (Shaoxing) or sherry

1 teaspoon sugar

1 teaspoon cornstarch

2 tablespoons safflower oil

6 garlic cloves, sliced

2 bunches watercress, washed, dried, and thick stems removed

1 Whisk together the soy sauce, wine, sugar, and cornstarch in a small bowl. Set aside.

2 Heat a wok over high heat until smoking. Add the oil. When the oil shimmers, add the garlic and stir constantly for 15 seconds. Add the watercress and stir-fry until it wilts, about 2 minutes. Add the soy sauce mixture and stir-fry for 1 minute more. Serve immediately. ✶

carrot and parsnip fries

serves 4

French fries but healthy! It's all about thin slicing and high heat to get the crispness and enhance the natural sweetness and savoriness of the parsnips and carrots. Parsnip is a highly underused vegetable. Shaped like a carrot, it has a unique earthy, savory-sweet taste.

3 medium carrots, peeled

3 medium parsnips, peeled

2 tablespoons extra virgin olive oil

½ teaspoon coarse salt

¼ teaspoon red pepper flakes

1 Preheat the oven to 400°F with a rack in the middle position. Halve the carrots and parsnips crosswise. Slice lengthwise into ¼-inch-thick planks, then slice into ¼-inch-thick fries.

2 Put the carrots and parsnips on a rimmed baking sheet and toss with the oil, salt, and red pepper flakes. Spread out into a single layer and roast, turning the veggies once, for about 20 minutes, until crisp and golden brown in places. ⋆

A Few Good Utensils

To execute this simple recipe, you need a good sharp knife and a firmly anchored cutting board.

maple-thyme roasted carrots

serves 4 to 6

I cook tons of carrots for my family. I always have a couple of bunches in the fridge, and they adapt to many different cooking techniques, making excellent sides for meats and poultry. Maple syrup and thyme accentuate their natural sweet flavor.

2 tablespoons extra virgin olive oil

2 tablespoons maple syrup

Leaves from 3 thyme sprigs

½ teaspoon coarse salt

1 pound carrots, peeled and sliced on the bias

1 Preheat the oven to 400°F with a rack in the upper third position. Mix the olive oil, maple syrup, thyme, and salt together in a medium bowl. Add the carrots and toss to coat.

2 Spread the carrots on a small baking sheet or in an ovenproof skillet and roast for 20 minutes, until tender and golden on the edges. Serve warm. ∗

NOTE

Cutting Your Vegetables One way to switch up your vegetable sides is to change the shape you cut them into—for instance, see Shaved and Steamed Broccoli (page 222). Carrots have many options: they can be shredded, julienned, sliced, or peeled and, if small, left whole. And there are plenty of options for how you slice carrots: coins, chunks, or use an oblique cut, as pictured opposite, to expose as much area to the heat and flavoring as possible. All this may seem like a big "duh," but it's these simple changes that keep vegetables a vibrant and interesting part of the plate.

mexican corn on the cob

serves 4

Starting in the spring, many New York City avenues are shut down for the day to accommodate the legions of vendors and food stands that populate the annual street fairs. One scent that stands out is the Mexican grilled corn. Walk through the fair, running into friends and neighbors as you munch on a hot piece of corn on the cob slathered in spiced cream, cheese, and fresh lime— a perfect afternoon slice of city life.

4 ears corn in the husk

1 lime

½ cup Mexican crema or sour cream

2 tablespoons chopped fresh cilantro

4 ounces queso fresco, crumbled

⅛ teaspoon chipotle chili powder

1 Preheat a double-burner cast-iron grill pan over high heat. (Or prepare a grill.) Peel the husks away from the cobs, leaving them attached. Cut 4 thin strips from a soft inner husk, and use them to tie the husks over the stalks. Remove the silk from the corn and rinse the husks under cold water to prevent them from burning when grilled.

2 Grate the zest from the lime and cut the lime into wedges. Stir together the crema, cilantro, and lime zest in a small bowl.

3 Grill the corn, turning occasionally, until the kernels are blackened in spots, about 5 minutes. Remove from the grill pan and slather with the crema mixture. Transfer to a serving platter and sprinkle the queso fresco and chili powder evenly over the corn. Garnish the platter with the lime wedges and serve immediately. *

OPPOSITE, FROM TOP: Creamed Corn with Jalapeño (page 234) and Mexican Corn on the Cob (above)

creamed corn with jalapeño

serves 4

I have a secret fondness for canned creamed corn, because my mom never bought it, but my friends' moms did. The jalapeño pepper gives this homemade version a Mexican twist. Eliminate the chili and change up the cheese if you want a more traditional flavor, with something like white cheddar or Muenster. **PHOTO ON PAGE 232**

2 tablespoons unsalted butter

1 shallot, minced

1 jalapeño, minced (seeds and ribs removed for less heat, if desired)

Two 10-ounce bags frozen corn kernels, or kernels from 2 ears

½ cup heavy cream

⅓ cup water

2 ounces Monterey Jack cheese, grated

½ teaspoon coarse salt

1 Melt the butter in a large straight-sided skillet over medium heat. Add the shallot and jalapeño and sauté until softened, about 2 minutes.

2 Meanwhile, puree one-quarter of the corn in a food processor or blender. Add the pureed corn and the remaining corn to the pan. Then add the cream, water, and cheese and stir and cook until the cheese is melted, 2 to 3 minutes. Season with the salt and serve. *

black-eyed peas

serves 6

My love of beans is no secret. I strive to serve a bean meal once a week. Black-eyed peas are eaten everywhere in the lower half of the USA. The peas, the basis for the lucky New Year's Day dish hoppin' John, also feature in the cold salad known as Texas caviar. And they're often found on a plate of Southern food together with their side partner Simmered Mustard Greens (page 226). If you don't have time to soak the peas overnight, use the quick-soak method for beans described on page 12.

1 pound dried black-eyed peas, picked over

1 meaty smoked ham hock

1 large yellow onion, chopped

3 garlic cloves, smashed and peeled

1 tablespoon coarse salt

2 bay leaves

1 Put the peas in a large bowl, add water to cover by at least 2 inches, and soak overnight in the fridge. Drain and rinse the peas.

2 Combine the peas, ham hock, onions, garlic, salt, and bay leaves in a large pot and add water to cover by 1 inch. Bring to a boil, reduce the heat, and simmer, stirring occasionally, until the peas are tender, 45 minutes to 1 hour. Remove from the heat.

3 Transfer the ham hock to a cutting board. When it is cool enough to handle, remove and discard the skin and bones. Chop the meat and return it to the pot. Reheat if necessary. Serve the peas directly from the pot using a slotted spoon. ∗

GOOD
TO
KNOW

Cooking Dried Beans Most recipes give a range of cooking time for dried beans such as black-eyed peas, because it's one thing you can't predict. Timing varies widely depending on the age of the dried beans, and when they are plucked from the grocery shelf. There's no way to determine how long they've been there. It's a different story if you buy beans from a known vendor at a farmers' market. Start tasting those beans for doneness at the lower end of the range.

japanese shredded cabbage

serves 4

I can't say enough good things about cabbage, an often overlooked veggie. It's inexpensive and a versatile chameleon that pairs beautifully with all types of ethnic dishes. Shredded and dressed with a lime-soy-sesame-oil dressing, it's a great simple salad. Serve with Pork Tonkatsu (page 161) and Cold Soba Noodles with Dipping Sauce (page 198) as part of a Japanese-style dinner. It's also a great accompaniment to fish. **PHOTO ON PAGE 162**

1 tablespoon white or yellow miso paste

2 tablespoons soy sauce

Grated zest and juice of 1 lime

2 teaspoons rice wine vinegar

1 teaspoon Asian sesame oil

¼ cup safflower oil

½ small green cabbage, such as napa or savoy, cored, quartered, and thinly shredded (6 cups)

Toasted sesame seeds (see page 17) for garnish

Whisk together the miso paste, soy sauce, lime zest and juice, rice wine vinegar, sesame oil, and safflower oil in a large bowl. Toss the cabbage with the dressing and serve, garnished with sesame seeds. ∗

MISO PASTE

Buy it, divide it, and keep it in your freezer. Miso paste is one of those ingredients that can really alter the flavor of a dish, adding that bottom "umami" flavor (or the "I can't put my finger on it" taste)—and not just in Asian cooking. Where you might add salty cheese, anchovy paste, or soy sauce to a soup or stew, stir in a spoonful of miso paste for a real flavor boost.

classic coleslaw

serves 6 (or tops 8 pulled pork sandwiches)

This is a simple, basic coleslaw. Serve it on the side with Brined and Fried Chicken (page 170) or pile it high on a pulled pork sandwich (see page 165) as a cool, creamy, crunchy counterpoint.

1 mild onion, such as Vidalia, halved lengthwise and thinly sliced crosswise

¾ cup mayonnaise

½ cup sour cream

2 tablespoons apple cider vinegar

1 teaspoon coarse salt

¼ teaspoon freshly ground black pepper

½ teaspoon celery seeds

½ medium green cabbage, cored, quartered, and thinly shredded (8 cups)

1 Put the onions in a bowl, cover with cold water, and let stand for 10 minutes.

2 Whisk together the mayonnaise, sour cream, apple cider vinegar, salt, pepper, and celery seeds in a large bowl.

3 Drain the onions and pat dry. Add to the bowl of dressing, along with the cabbage, and stir until well combined. Cover and refrigerate for at least 8 hours, or preferably, overnight.

4 Remove the coleslaw from the fridge 30 minutes before serving *

SOAKING SLICED ONIONS

If you are shy about using raw onions because of their pungent flavor, soak the sliced onions in cold water for 10 minutes. It pulls out some of the strong sulphur flavor notes and crisps them up in the process.

old-fashioned relish platter

serves 4

This relish platter—pickled beets, corn relish, and cottage cheese—is a facsimile of the one perched on a lazy Susan in the center of the table at the Midwestern roadhouse where I had some of my first restaurant meals. Fried perch or walleye pike (see page 178) was the featured attraction, and you filled up on the array of pickled vegetables and cheese while you waited. Many different pies, like Peach Pie (page 278), were in the wings for dessert! **PHOTO ON PAGE 179**

PICKLED BEETS

1 cup water

1 cup white wine vinegar

2 tablespoons coarse salt

¼ cup sugar

8 ounces beets, peeled, sliced lengthwise ¼-inch thick, and cut into matchsticks

CORN RELISH

2 ears corn, kernels stripped from the cob, or 2 cups frozen corn, thawed and drained

2 scallions, thinly sliced

½ red bell pepper, finely chopped

1 celery stalk, finely chopped

2 tablespoons white wine vinegar

1 tablespoon extra virgin olive oil

1 teaspoon coarse salt

¼ teaspoon freshly ground black pepper

1 cup (8 ounces) cottage cheese

1 For the beets, bring the water, vinegar, salt, and sugar to a boil in a small saucepan. Add the beets, remove from the heat, and let cool to room temperature.

2 For the corn relish, combine the corn, scallions, red pepper, celery, vinegar, olive oil, salt, and pepper in a medium bowl.

3 Transfer the beets, relish, and cottage cheese to serving bowls and serve. *

spirits & sweets

PRECEDING SPREAD: Candied Apples (page 281);
OPPOSITE, FROM LEFT: Negroni (page 252); Citrus Tequila Cocktail (page 253); Lychee Martini (page 244).

lychee martini

serves 2

This drink was inspired by A Single Pebble, one of the best Chinese restaurants I've ever eaten at, in the unlikely location of Burlington, Vermont. The syrup from the canned lychees is put to good use as part of the shaken mixture of vodka and vermouth. **PHOTO ON PAGE 242**

3 ounces vodka	Shake together the vodka, vermouth, and lychee juice in an ice-filled cocktail shaker. Strain into glasses, garnish with the lychees, and serve. *
1 ounce dry vermouth	
⅓ cup lychee juice (from canned lychees)	
2 lychees for garnish	

BUGABOO

While I'm willing to branch out from my favorite classic martini and try different versions such as this one, I'm adamantly opposed to commercially flavored vodkas. Every one tastes fake—like toothpaste or candy. Flavor the drink, not the spirit!

grapefruit thyme cocktail

serves 6

I created this drink for a birthday celebration while I was on a Jamaican vacation. Thyme and black peppercorns, local ingredients, steeped in a simple syrup. Grapefruit, which grows abundantly there, is used in a popular soft drink called Ting, and I think it adds the right "ting" in this drink too.
PHOTO ON PAGE 251

1½ cups water

1 cup sugar

½ bunch thyme, plus a few sprigs for garnish

2 tablespoons black peppercorns, crushed

Juice of 4 grapefruits

16 ounces vodka

Club soda

Cracked black pepper (optional)

1 Combine the water and sugar in a small saucepan and bring to a boil, stirring to dissolve the sugar. Remove from the heat, add the thyme and peppercorns, and let steep for 1 hour.

2 Strain the thyme and chill the syrup.

3 To serve, mix the grapefruit juice and vodka in a pitcher (this can be mixed ahead and chilled). Fill each of six 8-ounce highball glasses with 1 tablespoon of the thyme syrup, add ice to fill the glass, and fill three-quarters full with the grapefruit mixture. Top off with club soda. Garnish each with a sprig of thyme and some cracked black pepper, if desired. *

GOOD
TO
KNOW

The Spirit Revolution It's amazing what has happened to the traditional spirits of gin, vodka, and whisky. All sorts of small local distilleries have cropped up across North America, using regional ingredients for fermenting: maple, potatoes, pine, etc. Just as *terroir* defines a wine, so are these new spirits authentic representations of place. When you're traveling, pick up a spirit you've never tried and then create a memorable drink at home.

cape cod and collins jiggle shots

makes thirty-two 2-ounce shots

Here grown-up meets coed in a cocktail. More specifically, Mom gets schooled by her son Calder. Yes, these jiggly "shots" are usually the domain of bars in college-town USA, but those are made from neon-powdered Jell-O. Instead, we take a couple of classic cocktails and jiggle them up in a nod to college-party fun.

1¼ cups water

1 cup sugar

1½ cups lemonade

1½ cups pure cranberry juice (no sugar added)

2 envelopes unflavored gelatin

16 ounces vodka

Juice of 1 lemon

32 disposable 3-ounce plastic cups

1 Combine the water and sugar in a small saucepan. Bring to a boil, stirring until the sugar is dissolved. Keep warm, but don't let too much liquid evaporate.

2 Put the lemonade and cranberry juice in separate medium heatproof bowls and sprinkle 1 envelope of gelatin over each. Let stand until the gelatin softens, about 5 minutes.

3 Pour 1 cup of the hot simple syrup into the lemonade and stir until the gelatin is dissolved. Pour the remaining simple syrup into the cranberry juice and stir until the gelatin is dissolved. Add 1 cup of the vodka to each bowl and stir to combine. Stir the lemon juice into the lemonade mixture.

4 Place the plastic cups on a rimmed baking sheet. Divide the juices evenly among them. Cover with plastic wrap and refrigerate until set, at least 8 hours. The shots can be stored, covered, in the refrigerator for up to 1 week. *

GELATIN

Used to firm up liquidy mixtures, gelatin is one of those somewhat random ingredients like cream of tartar, yeast, food coloring, etc., that sit in the back of your cupboard collecting dust but are useful a couple of times a year. It's still worth the space it takes up for those times a recipe calls for it, such as molded frozen desserts or custards.

thrice-spiced bloody mary

serves 6

As my Arkansas-born colleague Regan taught me, there is no need to buy weird flavor-spiked tomato juice when you can infuse the juice yourself at home with, for example, an onion, a garlic clove, or a chili. If you're a Bloody Mary drinker, this will become your new favorite recipe. Spicy and deeply satisfying, it could almost be considered a salad! Yes, I'm lifting my ban on commercially flavored vodkas here. The pepper vodka is a must!

One 46-ounce can tomato juice

1 onion, halved

1 clove garlic, smashed and peeled

1 jalapeño

10 to 12 ounces pepper vodka

1 tablespoon Worcestershire sauce

½ teaspoon Tabasco or other hot sauce

¼ teaspoon freshly ground black pepper

1½ tablespoons prepared horseradish

Juice of 1 lemon

Garnishes: pickled okra, sliced cucumber, thinly sliced radishes, and/or celery stalks

1 Combine the tomato juice, onion, and garlic in a large pitcher. Cut a lengthwise slit in the jalapeño and add it to the tomato juice. Put the pitcher in the fridge and allow the flavors to infuse for at least a few hours, or as long as overnight.

2 To serve, stir in the remaining ingredients. Pour into tall glasses filled with ice, and garnish with the pickled okra and/or any of the other vegetables that you like. ⋆

spiked (or not) tarragon lemonade

serves 6

Simple syrup is an awesome way to customize your own cocktail flavors. The syrup, usually equal parts sugar and water heated until the sugar dissolves, readily absorbs the flavor of any ingredient steeped in it. There's something special about the combo of lemon and tarragon here. Without any alcohol, it's a great "soft" cocktail to serve; gin makes it "hard." **PHOTO ON PAGES 250–51**

1 cup sugar

4 cups water

Leaves from 6 tarragon sprigs, plus 6 sprigs for garnish

2 cups fresh lemon juice (from 10 to 12 lemons)

12 ounces gin (optional)

1 Combine the sugar and 1 cup of the water in a small saucepan and add the tarragon leaves, rubbing them between your palms. Bring to a boil, stirring until the sugar is dissolved. Let cool to room temperature. Strain out the tarragon.

2 Combine the lemon juice, tarragon simple syrup, and the remaining 3 cups cold water in a large pitcher. Refrigerate until ready to serve.

3 To serve, fill six glasses with ice. If using the gin, pour a shot over the ice in each glass. Add the lemonade and garnish each with a tarragon sprig. *

SIGNATURE COCKTAIL

Every summer, I experiment with different flavored simple syrups and other ingredients to devise a new cocktail. Just as in my cooking, I think about different ways to combine flavors and spirits, balancing sour, sweet, spicy, and salty. Stylized simple syrups are experimental and fun— an all-in-one way to infuse taste and sweeten the drink.

OVERLEAF, FROM LEFT: Cucumber-Mint Gin and Tonic (page 252); Spiked (or Not) Tarragon Lemonade (above); Grapefruit Thyme Cocktail (page 245).

cucumber-mint gin and tonic

serves 1

When summer hits, a G and T is one of my go-to cocktails, and Hendrick's gin is my brand of choice—it has a natural cucumber flavor note. Fresh cucumber muddled with mint enhances that flavor and makes a totally refreshing drink. **PHOTO ON PAGE 250**

3 mint sprigs

A 2-inch piece of English cucumber, halved lengthwise and thinly sliced crosswise

2 ounces gin, preferably Hendrick's

Tonic water

1 Strip the leaves from 2 of the mint sprigs and put in the bottom of a highball glass, along with the cucumber. Muddle (mash) with a muddling stick or the handle of a wooden spoon.

2 Fill the glass with ice, pour the gin over the ice, top off with tonic, and stir once. Garnish with the remaining mint sprig and enjoy. ✴

negroni

serves 2

Every time I drink a Negroni, I close my eyes and picture myself sitting at an outside table at a trattoria in a beautiful Italian city. A Negroni and its close cousin, the Americano, are both made with Campari, a fruit-and-herb-based aperitif originating in Novara, Italy (the Americano omits the gin). Campari has a slightly bitter flavor and also possesses digestive properties, making it an excellent appetite stimulant. This cocktail may also be served over ice in a short glass. **PHOTO ON PAGE 242**

1 cup ice cubes

2 ounces gin

2 ounces Campari

2 ounces sweet vermouth

2 orange twists for garnish

Put the ice in a cocktail shaker, add the gin, Campari, and vermouth, and shake well. Pour into two old-fashioned champagne glasses, such as coupes. Garnish with the orange twists. ✴

citrus tequila cocktail

serves 8

Remember the tequila sunrise, with its tonal gradation reminiscent of a Mexican beach scene? This is an update on that retro stalwart. Serve these, along with cold beer, when entertaining with Mexican food. **PHOTO ON PAGE 242**

2 cups orange juice

8 ounces tequila

¼ cup plus 2 tablespoons fresh lemon juice (from 2 to 3 lemons)

1½ ounces grenadine

3 cups club soda

8 strips lemon zest for garnish

1 Pour the orange juice, tequila, and lemon juice into a large pitcher. Tip the pitcher at a slight angle and carefully pour the grenadine down the side.

2 Divide the mixture among eight ice-filled glasses, and top off with the club soda. Garnish each glass with a strip of zest, and serve immediately. ∗

TEQUILAS

No need to splurge on expensive tequila for this one, as it is mixed with several other fruit flavors. A garden-variety white (blanco) or silver brand is fine. But, if you are so inclined, tequila is a lovely spirit to sip on its own. Try a reposado (aged at least two months), an añejo (aged one year), or an extra añejo (aged a minimum of three years). All are derived from the blue agave plant native to Mexico.

agua fresca

serves 4

Perfect when serving spicy Mexican food, it's delicious as is—or spiked with tequila. Use just one kind of fruit—don't mix them! A colorful array of different batches of this drink made from all kinds of fresh fruit and served in clear glass pitchers is a great display for a party.

4 cups chopped fresh fruit, such as cantaloupe, honeydew melon, watermelon, or pineapple

3 tablespoons sugar

2 cups water

Juice of 1 lime

Combine the fruit, sugar, 1 cup of the water, and the lime juice in a blender and blend until smooth. Pour through a fine-mesh sieve into a pitcher, using a rubber spatula or wooden spoon to help push all the liquid through the sieve; discard the fruit pulp. Add the remaining cup of water and stir to combine. Chill in the refrigerator until ready to serve. *

STREET FOODS

When you travel to another country or an ethnic community, check out the street food. In neighborhoods with a large Mexican community, for example, you'll find street carts packed with beautifully hued jars of agua fresca, ready to be served in Styrofoam cups over shaved ice. Tamale ladies sell their wares packed in coolers without ice so they stay warm. Taco trucks parked on the street corner offer tortillas with different favorite fillings. Street food, a direct connection with the people, is always the food everyone craves.

orange creamsicle float

serves I

Inspired by a famous soda in Philadelphia made with mandarin oranges and traditionally drunk alongside the steak bomb, Philly Cheesesteak (page 68). This is a drink, dessert, and old-fashioned popsicle all in one.

2 mandarin oranges,
or one 11-ounce can mandarin oranges

¼ teaspoon pure vanilla extract

2 scoops vanilla ice cream

Club soda

1 If using fresh oranges, remove the peel and pith. Suprême the oranges (see page 95) into a small bowl and squeeze the juice from the membranes over them. Or pour the canned oranges and juice into a bowl. Stir in the vanilla.

2 Transfer the oranges and juice to a tall glass. Add the ice cream and top off with club soda. Stir once and serve immediately, with a long spoon. *

REINVENT

Just as this recipe deconstructs, reimagines, and rebuilds the Creamsicle float, you can reinvent the Good Humor classic King Cone. Take the same ingredients and layer them into a parfait.

NUTSHELL RECIPE: **king cone sundae**

Crumble up a sugar cone and place half of it in a tall glass. Add a scoop of vanilla ice cream. Pour some hot fudge sauce (see page 286) over it. Sprinkle on chopped toasted pecans or walnuts. Repeat, and top with whipped cream.

OPPOSITE, FROM LEFT: Orange Creamsicle Float (above); Strawberry Buttermilk Shake (page 260); Chocolate Malt Milk Shake (page 258); Chocolate Egg Cream (page 259).

chocolate malt milk shake

serves 4

Chocolate and malt are an old-fashioned match made in heaven! This is the milk shake rendition of malted milk balls, my favorite candy. Serve with the Classic French Dip (page 66) for a full-on, full-calorie festival of flavor. **PHOTO ON PAGE 256**

1½ pints chocolate ice cream

2 cups milk

6 to 8 tablespoons malted milk powder, to taste

Combine the ice cream, milk, and malted milk powder in a blender and blend until smooth. Pour into tall glasses and serve immediately. *

MALTED MILK POWDER

Made out of barley malt, wheat, and milk, malted milk powder was originally created as a nourishing protein source for infants and invalids. Lightweight and long-keeping, this perfect packable also became popular for late-nineteenth-century explorers to take in their portable larders.

chocolate egg cream

serves 2

As a kid, I drank egg creams at the local delicatessen for several years before realizing there was no egg and no cream in them. What I love is the chocolate, natch—all fizzed up with seltzer water. It's a great foil for any salty deli sandwich. **PHOTO ON PAGE 256**

¼ cup unsweetened cocoa powder

⅓ cup hot water

½ cup light corn syrup

¼ cup sugar

1 cup milk

2 cups seltzer

1 Put the cocoa in a small saucepan, whisk in the hot water, corn syrup, and sugar, and bring to a boil over high heat. Remove the chocolate syrup from the heat and let cool to room temperature.

2 Stir together ⅓ cup of the chocolate syrup and ½ cup of the milk in each of two tall glasses. Top with the seltzer, stir once, and serve immediately. ＊

GOOD
TO
KNOW

Chocolate Syrup Chocolate syrup is the easiest thing in the world to whip together, and if you use a high-quality cocoa powder, the flavor is so much better than store-bought. Keep sealed in your fridge for a quick chocolate milk, hot cocoa, or mochaccino.

strawberry buttermilk shake

serves 4

Once in a while, a recipe comes together with a big "aha" moment. Searching for a low-fat, high-health alternative to my favorite milk shake, it occurred to me that the creamy acidity of buttermilk, replacing the whole milk, might be just the way to cut through the sweet, refreshing sorbet, which is used instead of ice cream. Serve this creamy, flavorful shake as part of my burger-joint redux health menu, with Chicken Chive Burgers (page 85) and Baked Potato Poppers (page 214). You can also customize your shake by varying the fruit sorbet. **PHOTO ON PAGE 256**

1 pint strawberry sorbet

2 cups buttermilk
(well shaken before measuring)

Combine the sorbet and buttermilk in a blender and blend until smooth. Pour into tall glasses and serve immediately. ✶

COLD AND FROTHY CAFÉ

vietnamese coffee shake

serves 6

This is a nouveau shake version of the traditional Vietnamese coffee—itself a result of the colonial French presence in Vietnam. The French brought coffee beans for cultivation to the country in the late 1800s, along with their tradition of *un petit café* in the morning. Chicory coffee, such as Café du Monde, is often used. Serve this along with a Banh Mi sandwich (page 82). Poured in small chilled cups, it's also a delicious dessert on a cool day.

2 cups strong brewed coffee, chilled

½ cup half-and-half

½ cup sweetened condensed milk

4 cups ice cubes

Combine the coffee, half-and-half, sweetened condensed milk, and ice in a blender and blend until smooth and frothy, about 30 seconds. Pour into tall glasses and serve immediately. ✶

GOOD
TO
KNOW

Guilty Pleasure Keep a can of sweetened condensed milk in the fridge. One spoonful of that cool, creamy sweetness is like a bite of candy, fudge, butterscotch, and ice cream all rolled up into one reverie-inducing indulgence.

black tea and citrus pitcher

serves 6 to 8

Your morning tea and orange juice combined into one brunch-worthy beverage. It's also a refreshing summertime drink to serve at a barbecue with smoky-flavored grilled foods.

3 bags black tea or
1 tablespoon loose tea leaves

4 cups boiling water

2 tablespoons sugar

1 lemon, halved lengthwise
and thinly sliced crosswise

2 cups fresh orange juice

1 Put the tea bags (or tea) in a large heatproof pitcher, add the boiling water, and let steep for 5 minutes.

2 Remove the tea bags (or strain out the tea) and add the sugar, stirring to dissolve. Stir in the lemon slices and orange juice, and refrigerate until cold.

3 To serve, pour into tall glasses filled with ice. *

vegetable-juice energizer

makes one 15-ounce drink

Although it can be very costly to buy your juice at a health food store, to DIY at home requires investing in a high-quality juicer—but if you like vegetable juice, it's worth it. To preserve the life of your juicer, get in the habit of washing and drying all the parts immediately after use.

1 pound carrots, tops removed

1 pound beets

1 bunch parsley

One 4-inch piece ginger

2 garlic cloves

Scrub the carrots well. Scrub the beets well and separate the bulbs and the greens. Set up the juicer with a small pitcher to catch the juice. Feed the vegetables (beet greens included), parsley, ginger, and garlic through the tube. Pour into a glass and drink immediately. *

Buy Your Vegetables Carefully Especially when I will be juicing fresh vegetables or eating them raw, I invest in organic ones. The flavor is better, and I don't have to wonder what suspicious chemicals might be conflicting with nature's medicine.

OPPOSITE: Greek Yogurt Cake (page 264)

greek yogurt cake

serves 8

This yogurt cake has a flavor and texture reminiscent of a delicious pound cake. The yogurt creates a moist yet delicate crumb, and the honey sweetens while adding a touch of floral flavor. Make the cake the night before, and it will still be moist the next day if well wrapped—a boon for the do-ahead needs of bake sales and potlucks. Serve with any fresh fruit topping, stewed dry fruits, or lemon curd.

2 cups all-purpose flour

2 teaspoons baking powder

½ teaspoon baking soda

½ teaspoon coarse salt

1 cup fat-free Greek yogurt

¼ cup honey

12 tablespoons (1½ sticks) unsalted butter, at room temperature

1 cup sugar

3 large eggs, at room temperature

1 teaspoon pure vanilla extract

Walnuts for garnish (optional)

Sour cherries in syrup for garnish (optional)

1 Preheat the oven to 350°F with a rack in the middle position. Butter and flour a 9-by-2-inch springform pan.

2 Whisk together the flour, baking powder, baking soda, and salt in a medium bowl. Stir together the yogurt and honey in a small bowl.

3 In the bowl of a stand mixer or in a large bowl using a hand mixer, beat the butter and sugar until pale and fluffy. Beat in the eggs, one at a time, beating until fully incorporated. Beat in the vanilla extract.

4 Add the flour mixture to the butter mixture in 3 additions, alternating with the yogurt and beginning and ending with the flour.

5 Transfer the batter to the prepared pan and smooth the top. Bake for 35 to 40 minutes, until the top is golden brown and a toothpick inserted into the center of the cake comes out clean. Cool the cake in the pan on a wire rack for 10 minutes. Remove the sides of the pan and invert the cake; lift off the pan bottom and let the cake cool completely.

6 Slice the cake and serve plain, sprinkled with sugar, or with the topping of your choice, such as walnuts or cherries. ⋆

EATING OUT

Yes, I'm first and foremost a believer in
home cooking. But meals eaten out hold a whole
different allure for me, and it's not because I don't
want to cook or enjoy my home. There is a rich
education to be had in a restaurant: manners,
decision making, communication, new food to
discover, culture, and the community around you.
From a barbecue shack to a fine-dining mecca,
memorable experiences await. Think of it as
a part of your family's life training. And take
the ideas home to weave into your
own history.

strawberries and cream chocolate birthday cake

serves 8 to 10

Sure, you can buy a cake from a bakery or the grocery store, but this cake is the quickest, most foolproof way to say happy birthday I know. It's my go-to cake when I need to pull a dessert from up my sleeve for someone's special day. The cake layers can be baked ahead, but assemble the cake just before serving. The cake pans do not need to be oiled or floured.

CAKE

3 cups all-purpose flour

2 cups sugar

¼ cup plus 2 tablespoons unsweetened cocoa powder

2 teaspoons baking soda

1 teaspoon coarse salt

¾ cup safflower oil or other vegetable oil

2 teaspoons pure vanilla extract

2 tablespoons white vinegar

2 cups cold water

FILLING

2 pints heavy cream

¼ cup confectioners' sugar

1 teaspoon pure vanilla extract

1 quart strawberries, washed, hulled, and thinly sliced

1 Preheat the oven to 350°F with a rack in the middle position. Whisk together the flour, sugar, cocoa, baking soda, and salt in a large bowl. Make a well in the center of the mixture, and add the oil, vanilla, vinegar, and cold water. Whisk until well combined.

2 Divide the batter between two 8-inch cake pans.

3 Bake the cakes, side by side, for 35 to 40 minutes, until a toothpick inserted in the center comes out clean. Cool completely in the pans on a wire rack.

4 Whip the cream to soft peaks in a large bowl. Add the sugar and vanilla and whip again until just stiffened; do not overwhip.

5 Slice the domed top off 1 cake round to make a flat surface and put it on a serving plate. Spread with a thick layer of the whipped cream. Top with a layer of half the strawberries. Top with the other cake round, domed side up, and spread it with another thick layer of whipped cream. Top with the remaining strawberries.

6 Slice and serve with any extra whipped cream and berries on the side. ✶

boston cream pie

serves 12

It's called pie, but let's face it, it's a cake—with an oozy, luscious pastry cream filling between moist layers and chocolate ganache dripping down the sides. It so gripped the taste buds of nineteenth-century Bostonians at the Parker House Hotel that it became a classic dessert—in fact, in 1996 it was named the state dessert of Massachusetts. A good way to tackle this cake is to make the cake layers and the pastry cream in advance. When ready to assemble, make the ganache topping.

CAKE

2½ cups all-purpose flour

½ teaspoon baking powder

½ teaspoon baking soda

1 teaspoon coarse salt

1 cup safflower oil

1½ cups sugar

4 large eggs, at room temperature

1 teaspoon pure vanilla extract

1 cup sour cream

PASTRY CREAM

1 large egg

4 large egg yolks

⅓ cup sugar

¼ cup all-purpose flour

1½ cups whole milk, heated

½ teaspoon pure vanilla extract

TOPPING

8 ounces semisweet chocolate, finely chopped

1 cup heavy cream, hot

1 For the cake, preheat the oven to 350°F with a rack in the middle position. Oil and flour two 8-inch round cake pans. Whisk together the flour, baking powder, baking soda, and salt in a medium bowl.

2 Whisk together the oil and sugar in a large bowl. Whisk in the eggs and vanilla. Add the flour mixture in 3 additions, alternating with the sour cream in 2 additions (beginning and ending with the flour). Divide the batter between the prepared pans.

3 Bake for 30 to 35 minutes, until the cakes pull away from the sides of the pans. Cool in the pans on a wire rack for 10 minutes, then remove from the pans to cool completely, right side up.

4 For the pastry cream, lightly beat the egg and yolks together in the bowl of a stand mixer fitted with the paddle attachment or in a large bowl using a hand mixer. Add the sugar a little at a time, and continue beating until the mixture falls in ribbons when the beater is lifted, about 5 minutes. Mix in the flour, then add the milk in a steady stream.

[Continued]

5 Transfer the mixture to a saucepan, bring just to a boil, and boil gently over medium heat, whisking, until the mixture thickens, 8 to 10 minutes. Strain the pastry cream through a fine sieve into a large bowl. Stir in the vanilla. Press plastic wrap against the surface. Cool for at least 1 hour.

6 For the chocolate ganache topping, put the chocolate in a medium bowl. Pour the cream over it and leave undisturbed for 1 minute. Stir gently, until the chocolate is melted and smooth. Let cool for 10 minutes.

7 Slice off the domed top of 1 cake layer to level it. With your fingers, remove some of the cake to make a ½-inch hollow, leaving a ½-inch border around the edge. Place on a cake stand or plate. Fill with the pastry cream. Top with the second cake layer, domed side up. Pour the topping over the cake, letting it run down the sides. Chill for at least 5 hours or as long as overnight, before serving. ∗

MASTER RECIPE

This white cake can be used with other frosting options for a killer layer cake. Dessert recipes often have components that will make an excellent basis for another dessert. Maybe you make a pie and realize the crust is amazing. A favorite pudding or custard could become a pie filling. Chocolate ganache drizzles hot over cream puffs, rolls into truffles, spreads on bread for a sandwich filling. Keep a file of your go-to recipe building blocks as you discover them and use them as the base for your own dessert creations.

independence day icebox cake

serves 8 to 10

It takes a patient decorator and a little time to pull off a big, beautiful holiday-themed icebox cake. Arrange the blueberries and raspberries on top of the strawberry-puree-spiked whipped cream to make the Stars and Stripes and celebrate the Fourth in style. But even if you scatter the berries recklessly, you will capture the rogue spirit of the USA!

One 12-ounce box vanilla wafers

1 pound strawberries, washed and hulled

3 cups heavy cream

⅓ cup sugar

1 cup blueberries

1 cup raspberries

1 Line the sides of a 9-by-3-inch springform pan with strips of parchment paper. Lay half the vanilla wafers on the bottom of the pan in overlapping concentric circles.

2 Puree the strawberries in a food processor.

3 Whip the cream to soft peaks in a large bowl. Add the sugar and whip again until just stiffened; do not overwhip. Transfer two-thirds of the whipped cream to another bowl. Fold the strawberry puree into the remaining whipped cream.

4 Put 1 cup of the whipped cream in a large resealable plastic bag. Snip off a bottom corner of the bag and pipe the cream over the wafers and around the inside edge of the pan to create a 1-inch-high dam. Pour the strawberry whipped cream into the center of the pan and spread it out level with the dam.

5 Arrange the remaining cookies over the cream in overlapping concentric circles. Top the cookies with the remaining whipped cream, spreading and smoothing it level with the edge of the pan. Arrange the blueberries evenly over one-third of the cream. Arrange the raspberries in four or five strips to create a flag pattern. Chill for at least 8 hours, or as long as overnight.

6 To serve, remove the sides of the springform pan and the parchment. Cut the cake into wedges. *

new york–style cheesecake

serves 12

"New York style" means heavy on cream—sour cream and cream cheese—for a decadent, swoon-worthy cheesecake that will send you to your fainting couch! The trick is to cook it enough to set without cracking the top. And don't cheat on the chill time. When you've come this far, you want perfectly set slices on your dessert plate.

CRUST

4 ounces graham crackers, broken into pieces

⅓ cup sugar

¼ teaspoon coarse salt

4 tablespoons unsalted butter, melted

FILLING

2½ pounds cream cheese
(five 8-ounce packages),
at room temperature

8 tablespoons (1 stick) unsalted butter,
at room temperature

One 8-ounce container sour cream,
at room temperature

1¾ cups sugar

5 large eggs

2 large egg yolks

Grated zest of 1 lemon

1 teaspoon pure vanilla extract

1 Preheat the oven to 375°F with a rack in the lower third position. Butter a 9-inch springform pan. Line the sides of the pan with 4-inch-wide strips of parchment, and butter the parchment.

2 For the crust, pulse the graham crackers, sugar, and salt to fine crumbs in a food processor. Add the butter and pulse until fully incorporated. Press the mixture evenly onto the bottom of the prepared pan. Bake for 15 minutes, or until the crust is golden brown and set. Transfer the pan to a wire rack to cool for 10 minutes. (Leave the oven on.)

3 For the cheesecake, in the bowl of a large stand mixer or in a large bowl with a hand mixer, beat the cream cheese, butter, sour cream, and sugar until light and smooth. Beat in the eggs one at a time, beating until fully incorporated. Beat in the egg yolks, zest, and vanilla extract.

4 Crisscross two 18-inch-long pieces of foil. Put the springform pan in the center of the foil and wrap the foil tightly around the bottom and sides of the pan to create a watertight seal. Transfer to a roasting pan. Pour the filling into the springform pan and smooth the top.

[Continued]

5 Pour enough boiling water into the roasting pan to come halfway up the sides of the springform pan and carefully transfer to the oven. Bake for about 1 hour 15 minutes, or until the top of the cheesecake is golden brown and the edges are set but the center still jiggles slightly. Remove from the oven and allow the cheesecake to stand in the water bath for 1 hour.

6 Lift the cheesecake from the water bath and remove the foil and parchment. Chill the cheesecake for at least 8 hours and up to 24 hours.

7 To serve, remove the sides of the springform pan and the parchment strips. Cut the cheesecake with a long thin-bladed knife. ✶

GOOD TO KNOW

Springform Pans One of these pans is a worthwhile investment if you're a cheesecake lover. But casseroles, quiches, deep-dish pizzas, and other cakes also love to be made in this deep pan with its removable sides, as does Greek Yogurt Cake (page 264).

chocolate mousse

serves 6 to 8

If I were allowed just one dessert choice for the rest of my life, it'd be some kind of chocolate-moussey type of thing, like this. Mousse sounds like it's a fancy, hard-to-make dessert, but it's little more than chocolate, cream, eggs, and sugar. Once made, it just requires some time to chill and firm up—so it's a good choice for a do-ahead dinner party dessert.

3 cups heavy cream

1 vanilla bean, halved lengthwise, seeds scraped out, and reserved, or 1 teaspoon pure vanilla extract

4 large egg yolks

3 tablespoons sugar

⅛ teaspoon coarse salt

8 ounces bittersweet chocolate, chopped and melted

1 Combine 1 cup of the heavy cream, the vanilla bean pod, and seeds in a 4-quart saucepan and heat until the cream simmers. Remove from the heat and discard the vanilla pod. (If using extract, stir it into the simmered cream.)

2 Whisk the egg yolks with the sugar and salt in a medium bowl until pale yellow and doubled in volume. Gradually whisk in ¼ cup of the hot cream and then add the egg mixture to the saucepan. Cook over medium heat, stirring constantly, until the custard thickens, about 3 minutes. Remove from the heat.

3 Whisk the custard and the chocolate together and let cool to room temperature.

4 Whisk the remaining 2 cups cream to stiff peaks in a large bowl. Stir one-quarter of the whipped cream into the chocolate custard, then gently fold the lightened custard into the whipped cream. Divide the mousse among custard cups or ramekins and cover with plastic wrap. Refrigerate for at least 4 hours, or as long as overnight.

5 Remove from the fridge 30 minutes before serving. *

Chocolate

Your mousse—or any chocolate dessert, for that matter—will strut its true point of view through your choice of chocolate. Nowadays the choices are almost overwhelming. You can go with the old familiar brands, but if you love chocolate, start tasting different varieties. Remember the places favorite bean flavors are from, and note the percentage of actual cocoa in a bar; the higher the percentage the more concentrated and "chocolatey" the taste is. Identify the attributes you love—floral, smoky, and herbal, for example—and pair the type of chocolate that matches the desired end result.

peach pie

serves 8

My mom is an excellent cook, but even she'd admit she never bakes. When I was growing up, it was the pie at the Rendezvous Tavern in Windsor, Ontario, that hooked me—so much so that I'll choose it over cake any day. Finishing our dinner meant we could pick a piece of our favorite pie: peach in summer, apple in fall, cherry in spring, key lime, pecan, or coconut cream in winter. Here's my own peach pie.

DOUGH

2 cups all-purpose flour

1 teaspoon course salt

½ pound (2 sticks) very cold unsalted butter, cut into pieces

½ cup cold water

FILLING

8 to 10 ripe peaches, peeled, pitted, and sliced

Grated zest and juice of 1 orange (⅓ cup juice)

¼ cup cornstarch

¾ cup sugar

3 tablespoons cold unsalted butter, cut into small pieces

1 egg, beaten with 1 teaspoon milk

1 For the dough, combine the flour and salt in a large bowl or a food processor. Add the butter and mix in (with your fingertips) or pulse until the mixture resembles coarse meal. Pour in the water and mix or pulse just until the dough comes together in a ball.

2 Cut the dough in 2 pieces. Wrap each one in plastic wrap and chill for at least 15 minutes. (If refrigerated longer, remove 15 minutes before proceeding with the next step.)

3 Preheat the oven to 375°F with the racks in the center and lower third positions. On a well-floured surface, roll out 1 piece of dough to a 12-inch-diameter circle. Fit it into a 9- or 10-inch pie plate. Trim the edges of the dough flush with the edges of the pie plate.

4 For the filling, combine the peaches, orange zest and juice, cornstarch, and sugar in a bowl. Pile the peaches into the dough-lined pie plate. Scatter the butter over the peaches.

5 Roll out the top crust to a diameter of 12 inches. Lay it over the peaches. Trim the edges of the crust so it extends over the bottom crust by at least ¾ inch. Tuck the top crust under the bottom and pinch together to seal. Crimp the edges with a fork. Chill the pie for a few minutes.

6 Brush the egg mixture over the crust. Cut a few slits in the top to allow steam to escape during baking.

7 Put a baking sheet on the lower oven rack to catch any overflowing juices from the pie. Put the pie on the center rack and bake for 60 to 70 minutes, until the crust is golden and the juices are bubbling. Cool on a wire rack for at least 1 hour before serving. *

individual tiramisu

serves 6

Tiramisu gets better with a little age. As the dessert sits, the separate layers meld together for a glorious symphony of flavor. But all tiramisus are not created equal—good-quality coffee, cocoa powder, and liquor make all the difference.

1 cup strong espresso

½ cup sweet vermouth or Marsala

4 large eggs, separated

½ cup plus 2 tablespoons sugar

1 cup mascarpone

36 ladyfingers

1 tablespoon unsweetened cocoa powder

1 Combine the espresso and vermouth in a wide shallow dish. Whisk the egg yolks with ½ cup of the sugar in a large bowl until pale yellow and doubled in volume. Whisk in the mascarpone until incorporated.

2 Whisk the egg whites with the remaining 2 tablespoons sugar to stiff peaks in another large bowl. Fold the whites into the yolk mixture in 2 additions.

3 Soak half the ladyfingers in the espresso mixture, turning once. Divide among serving glasses, working quickly so the ladyfingers don't become too soggy. Top with half the cream mixture. Repeat with a second layer of soaked ladyfingers and the remaining cream. Sift the cocoa over each tiramisu. Refrigerate overnight before serving. *

candied apples

makes 8 candied apples

Red Hots give the candied coating that classic cinnamon flavor and color. Use Granny Smiths, and you'll have an awesome contrast between green apple and candy-red color. You need to be careful when working with hot sugar, but the payoff is worth it. This is a showstopper of a dessert or treat for an after-school snack. You'll need a candy thermometer. **PHOTO ON PAGES 240–41**

2 cups sugar

½ cup light corn syrup

½ cup water

½ cup Red Hots or other red cinnamon candies

15 drops red food coloring

8 tart apples, such as Granny Smith, stems removed

8 candy apple sticks or wooden craft sticks

1 Combine the sugar, corn syrup, and water in a small heavy saucepan and gently stir with a fork over medium heat just until the sugar is dissolved. Raise the heat to medium-high and bring to a boil, without stirring. Add the cinnamon candies, insert a candy thermometer, and continue boiling, washing down the sides of the saucepan with a wet pastry brush occasionally to dissolve any sugar crystals. When the mixture registers 302°F (hard crack) on the thermometer, remove from the heat and stir in the food coloring. Let stand until the candy stops boiling.

2 Line a rimmed baking sheet with foil and coat with nonstick cooking spray. Insert the candy apple sticks into the stem ends of the apples. Carefully tilt the saucepan and dip each apple into the candy, swirling to coat the bottom and sides; allow the excess candy to drain back into the saucepan, and transfer the apple to the prepared baking sheet. Let cool and harden.

3 Candied apples are best served within 24 hours. *

Candy-Counter Inspiration

We all have it—our favorite childhood candy. One person's aversion (hello? licorice!) is another's addiction. Use your favorite candies as an ingredient or decoration—and as inspiration for a homemade dessert. Consider the flavors and textures you love in a candy and transform them. Recently a colleague baked what she called Irish coffee blondies. When I tasted one, I gasped with joy, because it tasted of my favorite childhood Canadian chocolate bar: Coffee Crisp. When I make the recipe, I'll call them Coffee Crisp Brownies.

bake sales

What on earth has happened to the humble, wholesome bake sale?

It's turned into a mini convenience store—tables laid with inferior packaged baked goods. How hard is it to make Banana Chocolate Chip Cookies (page 285) or a tray of Dark-Chocolate Peanut Butter Pretzel Squares (opposite)? I know it's tough with our crazy schedules, but more and more entities of all kinds—charities, schools, churches, sports teams—rely on this time-honored tradition to raise needed funds. It's supposed to be fun and delicious. Please join me in putting the "bake" back in bake sale. And, for heaven's sake, if you don't have time to bake, support the sale by purchasing a fresh baked good, not a packaged, preservative-laden impostor!

dark-chocolate peanut butter pretzel squares

makes 12 large or 18 smaller squares

My youngest son, Luca, called me one day from school and said, "Mom, we have a bake sale today for the soccer team and I need you to make something dank." Apparently the word "dank" now means something amazingly good. Being that it was last-minute, I was forced to be creative with what I had in the pantry: marshmallows, dark chocolate, peanut butter, pretzels, and puffed rice. His verdict? *"Mad* dank."

4 tablespoons unsalted butter

6 cups mini marshmallows

12 ounces (½ cup) crunchy peanut butter

6 cups puffed rice cereal

2 cups mini pretzels or pretzel sticks, broken into pieces

8 ounces dark chocolate, chopped (or semisweet chocolate chips)

1 Line a 9-by-13-inch baking dish with parchment paper, leaving an overhang on two opposite sides, and coat with nonstick cooking spray.

2 Melt the butter in a large pot over medium-high heat. Add the marshmallows and peanut butter and cook, stirring occasionally, until the marshmallows are melted and the mixture is combined and beginning to bubble, about 3 minutes. Remove from the heat and stir in the remaining ingredients until well combined. Scrape into the prepared baking dish and smooth the top with a spatula. Let cool to room temperature.

3 Use the parchment to lift the bars from the baking dish. Transfer to a cutting board and cut into squares. ✱

banana chocolate chip cookies

makes about 16 cookies

This is probably my sons' favorite cookie. When the kids were young, I started making these for them because I felt the banana was bringing a healthful bump to a cookie. Little did I realize the power the banana-chocolate flavor combo would have over the crumb-dusted faces of those smiling boys.

1 cup all-purpose flour

½ teaspoon baking soda

1 teaspoon coarse salt

8 tablespoons (1 stick) unsalted butter, at room temperature

¼ cup plus 2 tablespoons granulated sugar

¼ packed cup plus 2 tablespoons light brown sugar

1 large egg

1 teaspoon pure vanilla extract

1 very ripe banana, peeled and slightly mashed

¾ cup semisweet chocolate chips

1 Preheat the oven to 375°F with the racks in the upper and lower third positions. Butter two baking sheets or line with parchment.

2 Whisk together the flour, baking soda, and salt in a bowl.

3 In the bowl of a stand mixer or in a large bowl with a hand mixer, beat together the butter, sugars, egg, and vanilla. Add the flour mixture and stir to combine. Mix in the banana and chocolate chips until just combined.

4 Drop the batter by the tablespoon onto the baking sheets, spacing the cookies 1½ inches apart. Bake for 10 to 12 minutes, until lightly golden brown. Transfer to wire racks to cool. ✳

BANANAS

I buy bananas (organic) whenever I shop and keep the bunch in a bowl on the kitchen counter for anyone to grab and eat. It also means I have them in varying degrees of ripeness for baking and smoothie making. A smoothie just isn't right without the textural balance of a banana. And banana bread is a super-simple and beloved baked good to offer anyone. Need a quick dessert? Make banana splits with a couple of scoops of ice cream and some chocolate sauce (see page 286).

NUTSHELL RECIPE: **bananas flambé**

Sauté sliced bananas with butter and sugar. Flambé with rum by carefully igniting it to flame until it goes out. Drizzle with some cream.

hot fudge sundaes

serves 2, with sauce left over

Truth be told, ice cream is my all-time day-in and day-out guilty pleasure. But I can never keep it in the house, because the kids eat it all immediately. It's the only treat I covet that I can't hide from them. Cookies are in the sock drawer, chocolate bars in the produce crisper, but there's just no place for ice cream except the freezer. So, sundae making is a planned activity that I love. As for this chocolate sauce, I could (and do) eat spoonfuls of it straight out of the fridge for a chocolate fix.

5½ ounces semisweet chocolate, chopped (1 cup)

1 cup heavy cream

2 tablespoons water

1 tablespoon corn syrup

½ pint vanilla ice cream

2 fresh or jarred cherries

1 Put the chopped chocolate in a medium bowl. Combine ½ cup of the cream with the water in a small saucepan and bring to a slight simmer. Pour the cream mixture over the chocolate and allow to sit undisturbed for 1 minute. Stir until the chocolate is melted and smooth, then stir in the corn syrup until smooth.

2 Whip the remaining ½ cup cream to soft peaks in a small bowl.

3 Place 2 scoops of ice cream in each of two bowls. Spoon some sauce over the ice cream. Top with the whipped cream and a cherry. *

What to Do with Leftover Chocolate Sauce

- Heat and drizzle over pound cake.
- Spread on a cookie.
- Dip strawberries in it.
- Layer in a parfait.
- Spread over a refrigerator pie shell before adding the filling.

lemon icey

serves 6

A favorite summertime classic found at summer camps, on street corners, and at Popsicle stands. This frozen treat has a texture somewhere between an ice pop and sorbet, achieved by pureeing the ice crystals after they've formed. It's cool and bracingly refreshing.

1 cup sugar

1 cup water

1 cup fresh lemon juice (from 5 to 6 lemons)

1 cup ice-cold water

1 To make the simple syrup, combine the sugar and water in a small saucepan and stir over medium heat until the sugar dissolves. Remove from the heat.

2 Combine the lemon juice and 1 cup of the simple syrup in an 8-inch square glass baking dish. Transfer to the freezer and freeze, raking the mixture with a fork every 30 minutes, until flaky and frozen, about 3 hours.

3 Transfer the frozen mixture to a blender and puree with the ice-cold water. Divide among six 4-ounce ramekins or disposable paper cups and freeze until firm, at least 4 hours or up to 2 days.

4 Remove from the freezer 15 to 20 minutes before serving. *

KID IN US

strawberry lemonade popsicles

makes 16 ice pops

I was never in a park playground with the kids when they didn't beg for pops when the ice cream truck came around. Made with real fruit and no food coloring, these are a much healthier version. Swap out other berries or peaches for a change of flavor and color.

1 pound strawberries, washed and hulled

¼ cup sugar

2 cups lemonade

16 ice-pop molds

Combine the strawberries, sugar, and lemonade in a blender and blend on the lowest setting just until combined, with small pieces of strawberries still visible, 5 to 10 seconds. Divide the mixture among the ice-pop molds and freeze. *

EPILOGUE

by calder quinn

My first memories of eating are bowls of squiggly pasta with red sauce and lots of white cheese. My little self would devour everything put in front of me, but I'd always ask for more cheese—not satisfied until I had a heavy snowfall's worth of the white stuff blanketing every square inch of pasta. I would then mix it all up and ask for a top-off.

This fondness for cheese didn't strike me as peculiar until it was my turn to bring in the snack for my kindergarten class. My mom asked what I'd like to bring in. "Cheese," I answered. She returned from the store with a couple bags of that lunch-box staple, string cheese. "No, Mom," I said, "not that type of cheese—the hard cheese!" I meant Parmesan, which my parents kept in large chunks to be nibbled and grated. (Parmesan was literally my *only* indulgence—I was forbidden any type of sweets for a preposterously long time. Fast food was also banned at home.) This was my introduction to an interesting contradiction that arose whenever I ventured out of the safe cocoon of our apartment, where meals were made with good ingredients by two talented cooks who always put their love into everything they served.

The contradiction is: Raising your children on healthy, homemade, delicious food creates expectations that are impossible to meet when they venture outside the home. For many years I did not like hamburgers; hot dogs were okay, but I could not stand burgers. When I tried them outside they never lived up to the TV commercials, which made them look like epic sandwiches—two pieces of bun hanging on to fresh vegetables, melted cheese, and juicy meat for dear life.

In the fifth grade I began traveling to and from school unchaperoned. At first my parents gave me no money, but once I complained about the allowances given to the other kids, they relented

and I started receiving $2.50 a school day. This may not seem like much, but it was a bonanza for a ten-year-old tasting freedom for the first time—and ready to try all those foods that Mom and Dad didn't make at home.

I suppose it was inevitable that my first stop was the source of all those delicious commercials I had seen: a place where the smell of French fries, wafting toward my friends and me, announced its presence well before it was visible. I studied the red-and-gold interior as I waited in line behind my friends, eager to hear their orders. Chris asked the woman behind the counter for a double cheeseburger and fries, and Alec did the same, adding a "please." Now it was my turn: what else to do but follow the lead of my more experienced friends? As soon as we got our food, I bit into my very first double cheeseburger. Was it the best thing I ever tasted? No. Was it delicious and all the tastier because I paid for it myself and ate it sitting with my buddies? Yes. And so, as soon as I started eating outside my home, I became a wholehearted burger convert.

Similar food experiences soon piled up. If I managed to slip out of the house before oatmeal was forced on me, I had a bacon, egg, and cheese waiting for me on Broadway. When I wasn't spending lunchtime at the "ghetto Chinese" spot eating fried chicken wings and French fries doused in hot sauce, I was devouring slices of pizza barely recognizable underneath layers of oregano, hot pepper flakes, and, yes, Parmesan. Yet my mother never scolded me for my outside-the-house eating; she only insisted that I finish whatever was put in front of me for dinner. It would have killed her to know that I was spending my allowance on this crappy food, but I think she realized that I'd always return for her home-cooked meals.

In high school, my allowance was bumped up, but I started wanting that money for things other than food (hanging out with girls became a much bigger priority). This led me back to my parents' with my tail between my legs. I wanted to get packed lunches again. I don't know how I got so lucky, but even when I began taking my lunch to school, just like my little brothers, I managed to keep my daily allotment of five dollars. I thus learned another important lesson: food made at home was not only tastier than most of the stuff I got outside, but more affordable too.

Soon, I went off to college. Life in the dorms was a sea change. I'd been raised on my parents' cooking, more recently supplemented by the plethora of choices available on the streets of New York City. Access to a well-stocked refrigerator and kitchen was something I took for granted, but in my dorm I didn't have that anymore. Instead of just frying some eggs for myself, I had to go to the dining hall, swipe my meal card, and content myself with what they had to offer. I also became intimate with late-night takeout, and the attendant smell and taste of fast-food pizza and chicken wings, waking up many mornings with a stomachache and a wasteland of discarded cardboard boxes, greasy napkins, and squashed beer cans littered across the floor.

In dire straits, desperate for the taste of something homemade, I experimented with the meager options available in my tiny dorm room. An electric water boiler, some peanut butter, hot sauce, and packaged ramen noodles were all I needed to create a big bowl of peanut butter noodles (see Ramen Noodle Upgrade, page 139). On the electric

grill went bread and cheese (with some Cheetos layered in between) for grilled cheese after grilled cheese.

Those two years I spent without a kitchen created a gnawing deficit of homemade meals. As soon as I moved into an off-campus apartment, I dove in headfirst. Not one slice of pizza or a single chicken wing was ordered in for the first six months. Instead, I phoned my mother frequently to ask her how she made such-and-such, or what she did to make one dish so crispy and another so saucy. It was a huge learning curve, and in the process I learned how to balance a budget.

Feeding myself was just as important as spending money to hang out or party. I began cooking for, and with, my friends; our weekly sit-down dinners became a beloved tradition. It was a whole different experience from what I'd had at my parents' table, but the ingredients were the same: homemade food, good company, and lots of laughter.

Now that I'm an adult, I see clearly how the memories of my parents' kitchen shaped my life. Although I try to cook at home as much as possible, I still crave a slice of pizza and I know I will never make fried dumplings as good as those from my local Chinese spot. What I do know is that I love sharing my meals, whether made at home or eaten out, with the people I love. And I have my parents to thank for that.

ACKNOWLEDGMENTS

I want to thank the whole extended Mad Hungry family, especially Lauren Tempera; they've worked on all the MH projects: television, digital, products, and books.

Greg Lofts spearheaded this recipe work with me. Without him, this book wouldn't exist. At his side, Michelli Knauer has as big a heart as any cook I know. Caitlin Haught miraculously appeared and coordinated us all. My friend and creative collaborator James Dunlinson has managed this project from jump. His talent, generosity, and omnipresent good fun infuse every page. Photographer Jonathan Lovekin's understated, quiet grace produced irresistible food pictures. It was my privilege to work alongside an utterly pure artist.

Style props go to Rebecca Flaste Karson, my mom/sister, taste arbiter, and fellow mother of three boys. At Artisan, Trent Duffy kept the Mad Hungry train on the right track (and then some) and arranged for Judith Sutton to copy-edit this book—Judith taught me why she's legendary in the cookbook world. The designers of *Mad Hungry*, Jen Muller and Nick Caruso, devised a bold graphic style that I love; Michelle Ishay, Artisan's art director, took that design and evolved forward. Artisan's publisher, my beloved editor and collaborator Ann Bramson, is a unique and original bookmaker who makes my work so much better than I can by myself. Thanks are also due to her boss, Peter Workman, for all his support. I also appreciate the contributions at Artisan of Laurin Lucaire, Nancy Murray, and Barbara Peragine. The wisdom of Carla Glasser, my longtime agent and friend, keeps my books alive. My colleagues at Martha Stewart Living Omnimedia, a giant bubble of creative life force, provide immense support, inspiration, and advice.

The Scalas—mom, Rose, and brothers Jim, David, and Peter—planted the MH seed. My father, C. George Scala, would be be tickled pink if he had lived to witness the growth of his Mad Hungry gang. Finally, mad love forever to my nurturing Quinn family: Richie, Calder, Miles, and Luca.

INDEX

CONVERSION CHART

Here are rounded-off equivalents between the metric system and the traditional systems used in the United States to measure weight and volume.

WEIGHTS

US/UK	Metric
¼ OZ	7 G
½ OZ	15 G
1 OZ	30 G
2 OZ	55 G
3 OZ	85 G
4 OZ	115 G
5 OZ	140 G
6 OZ	170 G
7 OZ	200 G
8 OZ (½ LB)	225 G
9 OZ	255 G
10 OZ	285 G
11 OZ	310 G
12 OZ	340 G
13 OZ	370 G
14 OZ	400 G
15 OZ	425 G
16 OZ (1 LB)	450 G

VOLUME

American	Imperial	Metric
¼ TSP		1.25 ML
½ TSP		2.5 ML
1 TSP		5 ML
½ TBSP (1½ TSP)		7.5 ML
1 TBSP (3 TSP)		15 ML
¼ CUP (4 TBSP)	2 FL OZ	60 ML
⅓ CUP (5 TBSP)	2½ FL OZ	75 ML
½ CUP (8 TBSP)	4 FL OZ	125 ML
⅔ CUP (10 TBSP)	5 FL OZ	150 ML
¾ CUP (12 TBSP)	6 FL OZ	175 ML
1 CUP (16 TBSP)	8 FL OZ	250 ML
1¼ CUPS	10 FL OZ	300 ML
1½ CUPS	12 FL OZ	350 ML
1 PINT (2 CUPS)	16 FL OZ	500 ML
2½ CUPS	20 FL OZ (1 PINT)	625 ML
5 CUPS	40 FL OZ (1 QT)	1.25 L

OVEN TEMPERATURES

	°F	°C	Gas Mark
VERY COOL	250–275	130–140	½–1
COOL	300	148	2
WARM	325	163	3
MEDIUM	350	177	4
MEDIUM HOT	375–400	190–204	5–6
HOT	425	218	7
VERY HOT	450–475	232–245	8–9

★

FOR RICHARD QUINN